ELFIN D
2023

2023

January

M	T	W	T	F	S	S
						1
2	3	4	5	6	7	8
9	10	11	12	13	14	15
16	17	18	19	20	21	22
23	24	25	26	27	28	29
30	31					

February

M	T	W	T	F	S	S
		1	2	3	4	5
6	7	8	9	10	11	12
13	14	15	16	17	18	19
20	21	22	23	24	25	26
27	28					

March

M	T	W	T	F	S	S
		1	2	3	4	5
6	7	8	9	10	11	12
13	14	15	16	17	18	19
20	21	22	23	24	25	26
27	28	29	30	31		

April

M	T	W	T	F	S	S
					1	2
3	4	5	6	7	8	9
10	11	12	13	14	15	16
17	18	19	20	21	22	23
24	25	26	27	28	29	30

May

M	T	W	T	F	S	S
1	2	3	4	5	6	7
8	9	10	11	12	13	14
15	16	17	18	19	20	21
22	23	24	25	26	27	28
29	30	31				

June

M	T	W	T	F	S	S
			1	2	3	4
5	6	7	8	9	10	11
12	13	14	15	16	17	18
19	20	21	22	23	24	25
26	27	28	29	30		

July

M	T	W	T	F	S	S
					1	2
3	4	5	6	7	8	9
10	11	12	13	14	15	16
17	18	19	20	21	22	23
24	25	26	27	28	29	30
31						

August

M	T	W	T	F	S	S
	1	2	3	4	5	6
7	8	8	10	11	12	13
14	15	16	17	18	19	20
21	22	23	24	25	26	27
28	29	30	31			

September

M	T	W	T	F	S	S
				1	2	3
4	5	6	7	8	9	10
11	10	13	14	15	16	17
18	19	20	21	22	23	24
25	26	27	28	29	30	

October

M	T	W	T	F	S	S
						1
2	3	4	5	6	7	8
9	10	11	12	13	14	15
16	17	18	19	20	21	22
23	24	25	26	27	28	29
30	31					

November

M	T	W	T	F	S	S
		1	2	3	4	5
6	7	8	9	10	11	12
13	14	15	16	17	18	19
20	21	22	23	24	25	26
27	28	29	30			

December

M	T	W	T	F	S	S
				1	2	3
4	5	6	7	8	9	10
11	12	13	14	15	16	17
18	19	20	21	22	23	24
25	26	27	28	29	30	31

2024

January

M	T	W	T	F	S	S
1	2	3	4	5	6	7
8	9	10	11	12	13	14
15	16	17	18	19	20	21
22	23	24	25	26	27	28
29	30	31				

February

M	T	W	T	F	S	S
			1	2	3	4
5	6	7	8	9	10	11
12	13	14	15	16	17	18
19	20	21	22	23	24	25
26	27	28	29			

March

M	T	W	T	F	S	S
				1	2	3
4	5	6	7	8	9	10
11	12	13	14	15	16	17
18	19	20	21	22	23	24
25	26	27	28	29	30	31

April

M	T	W	T	F	S	S
1	2	3	4	5	6	7
8	9	10	11	12	13	14
15	16	17	18	19	20	21
22	23	24	25	26	27	28
29	30					

May

M	T	W	T	F	S	S
		1	2	3	4	5
6	7	8	9	10	11	12
13	14	15	16	17	18	19
20	21	22	23	24	25	26
27	28	29	30	31		

June

M	T	W	T	F	S	S
					1	2
3	4	5	6	7	8	9
10	11	12	13	14	15	16
17	18	19	20	21	22	23
24	25	26	27	28	29	30

July

M	T	W	T	F	S	S
1	2	3	4	5	6	7
8	9	10	11	12	13	14
15	16	17	18	19	20	21
22	23	24	25	26	27	28
29	30	31				

August

M	T	W	T	F	S	S
			1	2	3	4
5	6	7	8	9	10	11
12	13	14	15	16	17	18
19	20	21	22	23	24	25
26	27	28	29	30	31	

September

M	T	W	T	F	S	S
						1
2	3	4	5	6	7	8
9	10	11	12	13	14	15
16	17	18	19	20	21	22
23	24	25	26	27	28	29
30						

October

M	T	W	T	F	S	S
	1	2	3	4	5	6
7	8	9	10	11	12	13
14	15	16	17	18	19	20
21	22	23	24	25	26	27
28	29	30	31			

November

M	T	W	T	F	S	S
				1	2	3
4	5	6	7	8	9	10
11	12	13	14	15	16	17
18	19	20	21	22	23	24
25	26	27	28	29	30	

December

M	T	W	T	F	S	S
						1
2	3	4	5	6	7	8
9	10	11	12	13	14	15
16	17	18	19	20	21	22
23	24	25	26	27	28	29
30	31					

UNDERSTANDING THE INFORMATION IN THE DIARY PAGES

A guide to the astrological symbols

☉ Sun ☿ Mercury ♂ Mars ♄ Saturn Ψ Neptune

☽ Moon ♀ Venus ♃ Jupiter ♅ Uranus ♀ Pluto

ASPECTS

Each day, the Sun, Moon and other planets make aspects between themselves; these are known as mundane aspects. (In astrology 'mundane' doesn't mean 'dull', but refers to the word's original meaning of 'of the world', i.e. global rather than personal.)
 In the diary pages, each day's major mundane aspects and their times are listed on the left-hand page e.g. ♂☍♄ 20.15
In the example shown above, Mars is in opposition to Saturn at 8.15 pm GMT (the Diary uses GMT and the 24-hour clock throughout).

The basic meanings of these aspects are given below, but in order to understand their influence on your life more fully, it is helpful to know where the planets were at the time of your birth.

Aspects between the inner planets (Mercury, Venus and Mars) are common and have quite minor and fleeting effects. However, aspects between the outer planets (Jupiter, Saturn, Uranus, Neptune and Pluto) are quite rare and can have powerful effects on the whole community as well as on individuals.

I only use the major planetary aspects in the Diary, but astrologers also make use of the minor aspects - semi-sextile, quincunx, semi-square, sesqui-square, quintile, bi-quintile, septile, and novile. These can be useful in chart interpretations but their effects in mundane astrology are transistory at best.

ASPECT MEANINGS

Conjunction (0°) ♂

Harmonious or difficult depending on the planets involved. Each brings out the characteristics of the other. E.G. Moon conjunct Saturn will be difficult, Moon conjunct Jupiter will be harmonious.

Sextile (60°) ✶
Always harmonious, but not as powerful as a trine. Provides opportunity and openings - seize the moment!
Square (90°) □
The most difficult and challenging of aspects. Indicates obstacles, blockages and potential destruction. But you'll look back with pride on the achievements made at this time.
Trine (120°) △
The most harmonious aspect, provides good fortune and success with ease. That's if you can work up the energy to do anything - everything will appear so easy and effortless that you could lose the motivation to actually get going.
Opposition (180°) ☍
A difficult aspect, but not as powerful as a square. Indicates a need for co-operation and discipline. You'll be pulled both ways, so you will need to keep your balance.

HELPFUL AND UNHELPFUL PLANETS

A planet's characteristics will be modified according to its position in house, sign and its aspect with other planets. In any case, the nature of each planet is complex and to say whether its influence is easy or difficult is a great oversimplification. However, broadly speaking, and for the purpose of understanding the aspects, the action of the planets is as follows:
Helpful: Sun, Moon, Mercury, Venus, Jupiter, Uranus, Neptune
Unhelpful: Mars, Saturn, Uranus, Neptune, Pluto
You'll find more information on the planets and the signs in the following pages.

A NOTE ABOUT TIMES

All times given in the Diary are in the 24-hour clock format and GMT unless otherwise stated.
British Summer Time is currently from 01.00 on the last Sunday in March to 02.00 on the last Sunday in October. Just add one hour to get the BST times.

MAGICAL CORRESPONDENCES

MOON

Day Monday
Tarot Cards Moon, the Nines
Colours Lavender, Pale Blue, Pearly-White, Silver
Metal Silver
Gemstones Beryl, Black Onyx, Moonstone, Pearl, Quartz
Crystal.
Influences Astral Travel, Birth, Change, Children, Divination,
Dreams, Family, Feelings, Fertility, Hypnotism, Illusion,
Intuition, Mysteries, the Sea, Women's cycles.
Tree Willow
Plants Almond, Lily of the Valley, Lotus, Mandrake, Peony,
Water Lily.
Rules Cancer
Deities Aradia, Arianrhod, Cerridwen, Diana,
Creatures Boar, Cat, Dog, Fish, Hart, Hare, Horse

MARS

Day Tuesday
Tarot Cards The Tower, the Fives
Colours Brown, Burgundy, Dark Grey, Red, Scarlet.
Metals Iron, Steel
Gemstones Bloodstone, Chalcedony, Diamond,
Garnet, Red Topaz, Ruby.
Influences Courage, Death, Defence, Discipline, Discord,
Energy, Lust, Males, Problem-Solving, The Public, Renewal,
Revenge, The Self, Surgery, Wars, Willpower.
Trees Cedar, Furze, Holly, Oak
Plants Broom, Hops, Lily, Nettles, Rue, Thistle, Tobacco,
Woodruff, Wormwood.
Incenses Basil, Black Pepper, Clove, Coriander, Dragons Blood,
Galangal, Ginger.
Rules Aries, Scorpio (with Pluto).
Deities Aries, Macha, Mars, the Morrigu
Creatures Basilisk, Bear, Horse, Ram, Wolf

MERCURY

Day Wednesday
Tarot Cards Magician, the Eights.
Colours Orange, Slate, Violet, Yellow.

Metals Aluminium, Chromium, Quicksilver
(Mercury)
Gemstones Agate, Alexandrite, Cornelian, Opal, Sardonyx,
Topaz.
Influences Business, Communication, Drama, Education,
Employment, Exams, Information, Legal Matters, Logic,
Magic, Medicine, Prediction, Public Speaking, Science, Travel,
Writing.
Trees Hazel, Palm.
Plants Cinquefoil, Fern, Honeysuckle, Lily of the Valley,
Valerian, Vervain.
Incenses Benzoin, Dill, Frankincense, Lavender, Mace,
Marjoram, Vervain.
Rules Gemini, Virgo.
Deities Woden, Hermes, Math, Mercury, Merlin, Taliesin, Thoth.
Creatures Ape, Butterfly, Ibis, Snake, Swallow.

JUPITER

Day Thursday
Colours Blue, Purple
Tarot Cards The Wheel of Fortune, the Fours
Metal Tin
Gemstones Amethyst, Lapis Lazuli, Sapphire
Influences The Authorities, Career, Education, Honour,
Knowledge, The Law, Luck, Money, Philosophy, Politics,
Religion
Trees Ash, Cedar, Oak, Poplar
Plants Agrimony, Betony, Clover, Dandelion, Fir, Meadowsweet,
Shamrock, Verbena
Incenses Ash Seed, Benzoin, Carnation, Cedar, Olive Oil,
Styrax, Wood Aloe
Rules Sagittarius, Pisces (with Neptune)
Deities The Dagda, Danu, Jupiter, Lugh, Macha, Poseidon, Zeus
Creatures Eagle, Unicorn

VENUS

♀

Day Friday
Colours Green, Pink
Tarot Cards The Empress, the Sevens
Metal Copper
Gemstones Amber, Coral, Emerald, Jade, Lapis Lazuli,
  Malachite, Peridot, Rose Quartz, Turquoise
Influences The Arts, Beauty, Children, Fashion, Food, Friends,
  Love, Lust, Pleasure, Relationships, Young Women
Trees Birch, Elder, Myrtle
Plants Blackberry, Briar, Catnip, Coltsfoot, Rose, Sandalwood,
  Yarrow
Incenses Apple Blossom, Benzoin, Elder, Mint, Mugwort,
  Patchouli, Rose, Sandalwood
Rules Taurus, Libra
Deities Aphrodite, Arianrhod, Brigit, Freya, Rhiannon, Venus
Creatures Cat, Dove, Lynx, Sparrow, Swan

SATURN

♄

Day Saturday
Colours Aquamarine, Black, Dark Brown, Dark Grey,
  Indigo, Navy, Violet
Tarot Cards The World, the Queens, the Threes
Metal Lead, Pewter, Zinc
Gemstones Jet, Onyx, Sapphire, Turquoise
Influences Animals, Drama, the Elderly, Food, Grieving, Groups,
  Hardship, the Home, Land, Money, Old Age, the Old Religion,
  the Outdoors, Property, Studying, Success
Trees Alder, Elm, Holly, Yew
Plants Comfrey, Cypress, Fern, Horsetail, Ivy, Mullein, Reeds,
  Vines
Incenses Cypress, Dittany of Crete, Jupiter, Myrrh, Patchouli,
  Sandalwood, Cypress
Rules Capricorn, Aquarius (with Uranus)
Deities Arianrhod, Branwen, Cerridwen, Cybele, the Morrigu,
  Persephone, Saturn
Creatures Crocodile, Dragon, Goat, Woman

SUN

Day Sunday
Colours Orange, Yellow, Gold, Rust
Tarot Cards   The Sun, the Knights, the Sixes
Metal Gold
Gemstones Topaz, Diamond, Amber, Carnelian, Ruby
Influences Confidence, Diplomacy, Friendship, Health, Jewels, Money, Peace, Power, Prosperity, Status, Success
Trees Laurel, Birch, Elm, Vine, Ash
Plants Chamomile, Chicory, Heliotrope, Marigold, Mistletoe, Rose, Rue, St. John's Wort, Sunflower
Incenses Bay, Cinnamon, Frankincense, Orange, Saffron
Rules Leo
Deities Adonis, Apollo, Bel, Bran, the Dagda, Mithras, Osiris, Ra
Creatures Child, Hawk, Lion, Peacock, Phoenix, Snake

ARIES

Day Tuesday
Number 9
Tarot card The Emperor
Keywords Courage, Will, Self Focus, Confident, Initiate, First, Hunter, Enthusiasm, Inspiration, Vital, Mission, Conquer, Activation
Colours Dark red
Ruling planet Mars
Quality Cardinal
Element Fire
Body parts Head. Face, Adrenal Gland
Metal Iron
Gemstones Bloodstone, Diamond, Garnet
Incense Dragon's Blood
Plants Sage, Allspice, Cinnamon, Cloves, Nettles, Thistle
Trees Hawthorn, holly, spruce, all thorny trees/shrubs
Creatures Ram, Robin, Tiger

TAURUS

Day Friday

Number 6

Tarot card The Hierophant

Keywords Pleasure, Solid, Stable, Security, Possessions, Money, Beauty, Loyal, Stubborn, Sensual, Practical, Patient, Indulgent, Enduring, Storage, Regulating

Colours Green, Yellow

Ruling planet Venus

Quality Fixed

Element Earth

Body parts Throat, Neck, Thyroid Gland, Vocal Cords, Ears

Metal Copper

Gemstones Emerald, Jade, Malachite

Incense Storax

Plants Honeysuckle, Mint, Sorrel, Sage Thyme, Foxglove, Rose, Poppy, Daisy, Violet, Dandelion

Trees Cypress, Ash, Apple, Pear, Fig

Creatures All Cattle

GEMINI

Day Wednesday

Number 5

Tarot cards The Magician, The Lovers

Keywords Curious, Inquisitive, Intelligent, Witty, Cheeky Mischievous, Communication, Perception, Learning

Colours White, Yellow, Orange, Light Blue

Ruling planet Mercury

Quality Mutable

Element Air

Body parts Shoulders, Arms, Hands, Lungs, Nervous System, Thymus Gland

Metal Mercury

Gemstones Agate, Citrine, Tiger's Eye, Peridot

Incense Jasmine, Sandalwood

Plants Lily of the Valley, Lavender, Fern, Myrtle

Trees Hazel, Horse Chestnuts, All Nut-Bearing Trees

Creatures Magpies, Parrots, Monkeys, Butterflies, All Small Birds

CANCER

Day Monday
Number 2
Tarot card The Chariot
Keywords Sensitive, Nurturing, Intuitive, Selfless, Giving, Caring, Protective, Moody, Receptive, Enfolding, Containment
Colours White, Silver
Ruling planet Moon
Quality Cardinal
Element Water
Body parts Breasts, Stomach
Metal Silver
Gemstones Moonstone, Pearl
Incense Sadnalwood
Plants White Rose, Water Lily, Lotus, Eucalyptus, Milkweed, Lemon
Trees Alder, Willow, Acanthus
Creatures Frogs, Crabs, All Crustaceans

LEO

Day Sunday
Number 1
Tarot card Strength
Keywords Artistic, Dramatic, Regal, Proud, Leadership, Performer, Expressive, Creative, Concentration, Glowing, Personality
Colours Gold, Orange, Yellow
Ruling planet Sun
Quality Fixed
Element Fire
Body parts Heart, Spine, Lower Back
Metal Gold
Gemstones Ruby, Cats Eye
Incense Frankincense
Plants Celandine, Sunflower, Marigold, Saffron, St Johns Wort
Trees Bay, Olive, Laurel, Walnut, Citrus Trees
Creatures Cats, Wolves, Lions

VIRGO

Day Wednesday
Number 5
Tarot card The Hermit
Keywords Systematic, Ordered, Purifying, Analytical, Process Orientated, Practical, Precise, Discriminating, Critical
Colours White, Purple
Ruling planet Mercury
Quality Mutable
Element Earth
Body parts Intestines, Lower Digestive System, Spleen
Metal Platinum, Nickel
Gemstones Amazonite, Amethyst, Charoite, Peridot
Incense Narcissus
Plants Flax, Buttercup, Lavender, Forget-Me-Not, All Small Flowers
Trees Hazel, Elder, Cypress
Creatures Squirrels, Mice, Insects, Bees, All Domestic Pets

LIBRA

Day Friday
Number 6
Tarot card Justice
Keywords Art, Beauty, Harmony, Peace, Relationship, Debate, Cooperation, Diplomacy, Compromise, Mediator, Peacemaker, Justice, Fairness, Balancing, Sharing, Partnership
Colours Pale Blue, Pink, Green
Ruling planet Venus
Quality Cardinal
Element Air
Body parts Kidney, Lower Back, Endocrine System
Metal Aluminium, Bronze, Copper
Gemstones Jade, Sapphire, Topaz
Incense Galbanum
Plants Catnip, Majoram, Sweet Pea, Roses, Hydrangeas, Daisies, Dahlias
Trees Ash, Poplar, White Sycamore, Fig
Creatures Elephant, Salmon, Snakes, Lizards

SCORPIO

Day Tuesday
Number 9
Tarot card Death
Keywords Focused, Driven, Ambitious, Emotionally Intense,
Persistence, Determination, Desire, Depth, Magnetic, Purifying
Colours Black, Maroon
Ruling planets Pluto, Mars
Quality Fixed
Element Water
Body parts Bladder, Genitals, Reproductive System
Metal Iron, Steel, Plutonium
Gemstones Opal, Obsidian
Incense Benzoin
Plants Geraniums, Rhododendrons, Honeysuckle, Heather,
Gentian
Trees Hawthorn, Blackthorn, Bramble, Witch Hazel, Birch
Creatures Scorpions, Eagles, Scarab Beetles, Dogs

SAGITTARIUS

Day Thursday
Number 3
Tarot card Temperance
Keywords Travel, Higher Learning, Thirst for New Experiences,
Philosophical, Questing, Seeking, Teaching
Colours Royal Blue, Purple, Brown
Ruling planet Jupiter
Quality Mutable
Element Fire
Body parts Hips, Thighs, Liver, Pituitary Gland
Metal Tin, Brass
Gemstones Topaz, Labradorite, Smokey Quartz
Incense Cinnamon
Plants Dandelions, Thistle, Carnations, Horsetail, Wood Betony,
Mallow
Trees Ash, Silver Birch, Oak, Mulberry, Chestnut, Lime
Creatures Horses, Stags, All Hunted Animals

CAPRICORN

Day Saturday
Number 8
Tarot card The Devil
Keywords hardworking, diligent, practical, ambitious, loner, prudent, conservative, economical, achievement, goals, structural, efficiency of resources
Colours Dark Green, Grey, Black, Brown
Ruling planet Saturn
Quality Cardinal
Element Earth
Body parts Knees, Skin, Skeleton, Teeth
Metal Lead, Pewter
Gemstones Onyx
Incense Musk
Plants Hemlock, Comfrey, Henbane, Pansy, Ivy, Poppy, Hellebore, Horsetail
Trees Willow, Pine, Elm, Yew, Aspen, Poplar
Creatures Pigs, Goats, All Cloven-Hoofed Animals

AQUARIUS

Day Saturday
Number 4
Tarot card The Star
Keywords Detached, Intelligent, Social, Rebellious, Individual, Unorthodox, Logical, Team, Utopia, Groups
Colours Sky Blue, Turquoise
Ruling planets Uranus, Saturn
Quality Fixed
Element Air
Body parts Shins, Circulatory System, Ankles, Pineal Gland
Metal Aluminium, Uranium
Gemstones Aquamarine, Lapis Lazuli
Incense Galbanum
Plants Orchid, Passion Flower, Hops, Mandrake
Trees Elder, Frankincense, Myrrh, Rowan
Creatures Peacocks, Albatrosses, All Birds That Fly Long Distances

14

PISCES

Day Thursday
Number 7
Tarot card The Moon
Keywords Adaptable, Compassionate, Psychic, Creative, Spiritual, Escapist, Dreamer, Subjective, Imagination, Diffusion
Colours Sea Green, Blue, Indigo
Ruling planets Neptune, Jupiter
Quality Mutable
Element Water
Body parts Pituitary Gland, Lymphatic System, Immune System, Feet
Metal Tin
Gemstones Moonstone, Pearl, Bloodstone
Incense Orris Root
Plants Water Lily, Moss, Ferns, Iris, Evening Primrose, Plants That Grow by Water
Trees Willow
Creatures Fish, All Sea Mammals

DATES OF RETROGRADE PLANETS 2023

MERCURY Until 18th January (in Capricorn); 21st April - 15thMay (in Taurus); 23rd August - 16th September (in Virgo); 13th December - 1st January 2024 (in Capricorn/ Sagittarius)

VENUS 23rd July - 4th September (in Leo)

MARS Until 12th January (in Gemini)

JUPITER 4th September - 31st December (in Taurus)

SATURN 17th June - 4th November (in Pisces)

URANUS 29th August - 27th January 2024 (in Taurus)

NEPTUNE 30th June - 6th December (in Pisces)

PLUTO 1st May - 11th October (in Aquarius/Capricorn)

PLANETARY HOURS

Using Planetary Hours for Magical Purposes

If you wish to work magic, or meditate, for a particular purpose, what are the best times for a successful outcome?

For magical and divination purposes, the whole 24-hour day is divided into 2 blocks of 12 hours each. The 'day' block is measured from sunrise to sunset and the 'night' block is measured from sunset to sunrise; each block is evenly divided into 12 'hours' Each of these 'hours' has its own ruling planet and each day of the week has its own set of planetary rulerships.

Generally, daytime workings are for positive outcomes, nighttime working are for negative purposes. Once you have decided which planet suits your purpose (see The Meanings of the Planets overleaf), you can use the table to help you find the best time.

Here is an example:
Suppose you want to work a spell for success in a legal matter. The law is covered by Jupiter, so choose Jupiter's day which is Thursday. This is a positive spell, so look in the daytime table and choose an hour that belongs to Jupiter - such as the 1st hour. Choose a suitable date - Thursday 6th January 2022, say - and look up the sunrise and sunset times (page 33).* Sunrise on that date is at 8.05 and sunset is at 16.08; the time interval between them is 7 hours and 57 minutes. Dividing by 12 gives you an 'hour' of 40 minutes. Since you want the first hour (the Jupiter hour), you have between 8.05 and 8.45 to work your spell.

*The sunrise/sunset times given in the Diary are for London and SE England only; for other locations, use a website such as www.timeanddate.com. And remember that all times given in the Diary are for GMT; add an hour for BST.

Table of Planetary Hour Rulers

Day Hours (Sunrise to Sunset)

	1	2	3	4	5	6	7	8	9	10	11	12
S	☉	♀	☿	☽	♄	♃	♂	☉	♀	☿	☽	♄
M	☽	♄	♃	♂	☉	♀	☿	☽	♄	♃	♂	☉
T	♂	☉	♀	☿	☽	♄	♃	♂	☉	♀	☿	☽
W	☿	☽	♄	♃	♂	☉	♀	☿	☽	♄	♃	♂
T	♃	♂	☉	♀	☿	☽	♄	♃	♂	☉	♀	☿
F	♀	☿	☽	♄	♃	♂	☉	♀	☿	☽	♄	♃
S	♄	♃	♂	☉	♀	☿	☽	♄	♃	♂	☉	♀

Night Hours (Sunset to Sunrise)

	1	2	3	4	5	6	7	8	9	10	11	12
S	♃	♂	☉	♀	☿	☽	♄	♃	♂	☉	♀	☿
M	♀	☿	☽	♄	♃	♂	☉	♀	☿	☽	♄	♃
T	♄	♃	♂	☉	♀	☿	☽	♄	♃	♂	☉	♀
W	☉	♀	☿	☽	♄	♃	♂	☉	♀	☿	☽	♄
T	☽	♄	♃	♂	☉	♀	☿	☽	♄	♃	♂	☉
F	♂	☉	♀	☿	☽	♄	♃	♂	☉	♀	☿	☽
S	☿	☽	♄	♃	♂	☉	♀	☿	☽	♄	♃	♂

Planetary symbols:
♀- Venus; ☿ - Mercury; ☽ - Moon; ♄ - Saturn; ♃ - Jupiter;
♂ - Mars; ☉ - Sun

JANUARY 2023 set for midnight GMT

Day	Sid.t	☉	☽	☿	♀	♂	♃	♄	♅	♆	♇	☊	☊
S 1	6 41 33	10♑17'02	3♉39	23°R42	27♑23	9°R 4	1♈12	22♒25	15°R 9	22♓52	27♑39	11♉45	10♉12
M 2	6 45 30	11°18'10	16°14	23♑ 6	28°38	8♊55	1°19	22°31	15♉ 8	22°53	27°41	11°R45	10° 9
T 3	6 49 26	12°19'19	28°36	22°18	29°53	8°46	1°26	22°37	15° 7	22°54	27°43	11°44	10° 6
W 4	6 53 23	13°20'27	10♊48	21°20	1♒ 8	8°39	1°34	22°43	15° 6	22°55	27°45	11°40	10° 3
T 5	6 57 20	14°21'35	22°53	20°13	2°23	8°32	1°42	22°49	15° 5	22°56	27°47	11°33	10° 0
F 6	7 1 16	15°22'43	4♋52	18°59	3°39	8°26	1°50	22°56	15° 4	22°57	27°49	11°23	9°56
S 7	7 5 13	16°23'51	16°47	17°40	4°54	8°21	1°58	23° 2	15° 3	22°59	27°51	11°11	9°53
S 8	7 9 9	17°24'59	28°41	16°20	6° 9	8°17	2° 6	23° 8	15° 2	23° 0	27°53	10°58	9°50
M 9	7 13 6	18°26'06	10♌33	15° 0	7°24	8°14	2°14	23°15	15° 2	23° 1	27°55	10°45	9°47
T 10	7 17 2	19°27'14	22°26	13°42	8°39	8°11	2°23	23°21	15° 1	23° 2	27°57	10°32	9°44
W11	7 20 59	20°28'21	4♍21	12°31	9°54	8° 9	2°32	23°28	15° 0	23° 3	27°59	10°21	9°40
T 12	7 24 55	21°29'29	16°21	11°26	11° 9	8° 8	2°40	23°34	15° 0	23° 5	28° 1	10°13	9°37
F 13	7 28 52	22°30'36	28°30	10°30	12°24	8°D 8	2°49	23°41	14°59	23° 6	28° 3	10° 8	9°34
S 14	7 32 49	23°31'43	10♎51	9°42	13°39	8° 8	2°58	23°47	14°59	23° 7	28° 5	10° 5	9°31
S 15	7 36 45	24°32'50	23°29	9° 5	14°54	8° 9	3° 8	23°54	14°58	23° 9	28° 7	10°D 5	9°28
M1	7 40 42	25°33'57	6♏28	8°37	16° 9	8°11	3°17	24° 0	14°58	23°10	28° 9	10°R 5	9°25
T 17	7 44 38	26°35'03	19°53	8°19	17°24	8°14	3°26	24° 7	14°57	23°11	28°11	10° 4	9°21
W18	7 48 35	27°36'10	3♐47	8° 9	18°39	8°18	3°36	24°14	14°57	23°13	28°12	10° 3	9°18
T 19	7 52 31	28°37'17	18°10	8°D 9	19°54	8°22	3°46	24°21	14°57	23°14	28°14	9°58	9°15
F 20	7 56 28	29°38'23	3♑ 0	8°17	21° 8	8°27	3°56	24°27	14°57	23°16	28°16	9°51	9°12
S 21	8 0 24	0♒39'29	18°11	8°32	22°23	8°32	4° 6	24°34	14°57	23°17	28°18	9°41	9° 9
S 22	8 4 21	1°40'34	3♒32	8°54	23°38	8°39	4°16	24°41	14°56	23°19	28°20	9°30	9° 6
M2	8 8 18	2°41'38	18°53	9°22	24°53	8°46	4°26	24°48	14°D56	23°21	28°22	9°18	9° 2
T 24	8 12 14	3°42'42	4♓ 0	9°56	26° 8	8°53	4°36	24°55	14°56	23°22	28°24	9° 8	8°59
W25	8 16 11	4°43'44	18°46	10°35	27°23	9° 2	4°47	25° 2	14°57	23°24	28°26	8°59	8°56
T 26	8 20 7	5°44'46	3♈ 3	11°19	28°37	9°10	4°57	25° 9	14°57	23°25	28°28	8°54	8°53
F 27	8 24 4	6°45'46	16°51	12° 7	29°52	9°20	5° 8	25°16	14°57	23°27	28°30	8°51	8°50
S 28	8 28 0	7°46'45	0♉10	12°58	1♓ 7	9°30	5°19	25°23	14°57	23°29	28°32	8°50	8°46
S 29	8 31 57	8°47'44	13° 3	13°54	2°21	9°41	5°30	25°30	14°57	23°31	28°34	8°50	8°43
M3	8 35 53	9°48'41	25°35	14°52	3°36	9°52	5°41	25°37	14°58	23°32	28°36	8°49	8°40
T 31	8 39 50	10♒49'37	7♊51	15♑53	4♓51	10♊ 4	5♈52	25♒44	14♉58	23♓34	28♑38	8♉47	8♉37

FEBRUARY 2023 set for midnight GMT

Day	Sid.t	☉	☽	☿	♀	♂	♃	♄	⛢	♆	♇	☊	☊
W 1	8 43 47	11♒50'31	19Ⅱ56	16♑57	6✶ 5	10Ⅱ17	6♈ 3	25♒51	14♉59	23✶36	28♑40	8♌R42	8♌34
T 2	8 47 43	12♒51'25	1♋54	18° 3	7°20	10°30	6°15	25°58	14°59	23°38	28°42	8°35	8°31
F 3	8 51 40	13°52'17	13°47	19°12	8°34	10°43	6°26	26° 5	15° 0	23°40	28°44	8°24	8°27
S 4	8 55 36	14°53'08	25°39	20°22	9°49	10°57	6°38	26°13	15° 0	23°41	28°46	8°11	8°24
S 5	8 59 33	15°53'58	7♌31	21°35	11° 3	11°12	6°49	26°20	15° 1	23°43	28°48	7°56	8°21
M 6	9 3 29	16°54'46	19°25	22°49	12°18	11°27	7° 1	26°27	15° 2	23°45	28°49	7°41	8°18
T 7	9 7 26	17°55'34	1♍23	24° 4	13°32	11°43	7°13	26°34	15° 2	23°47	28°51	7°27	8°15
W 8	9 11 22	18°56'20	13°25	25°21	14°46	11°59	7°25	26°41	15° 3	23°49	28°53	7°15	8°12
T 9	9 15 19	19°57'05	25°32	26°40	16° 1	12°15	7°37	26°48	15° 4	23°51	28°55	7° 6	8° 8
F 10	9 19 16	20°57'49	7♎48	28° 0	17°15	12°32	7°49	26°56	15° 5	23°53	28°57	7° 0	8° 5
S 11	9 23 12	21°58'32	20°13	29°21	18°29	12°49	8° 1	27° 3	15° 6	23°55	28°59	6°56	8° 2
S 12	9 27 9	22°59'14	2♏53	0♒43	19°43	13° 7	8°13	27°10	15° 7	23°57	29° 1	6♌D55	7°59
M 13	9 31 5	23°59'54	15°50	2° 7	20°58	13°25	8°25	27°17	15° 8	23°59	29° 2	6°55	7°56
T 14	9 35 2	25° 0'34	29° 9	3°32	22°12	13°44	8°38	27°25	15° 9	24° 1	29° 4	6♌R55	7°52
W 15	9 38 58	26° 1'13	12♐51	4°57	23°26	14° 3	8°50	27°32	15°10	24° 3	29° 6	6°54	7°49
T 16	9 42 55	27° 1'51	27° 0	6°24	24°40	14°22	9° 3	27°39	15°12	24° 5	29° 8	6°51	7°46
F 17	9 46 51	28° 2'27	11♑34	7°52	25°54	14°42	9°15	27°46	15°13	24° 7	29°10	6°45	7°43
S 18	9 50 48	29° 3'02	26°30	9°21	27° 8	15° 2	9°28	27°54	15°14	24° 9	29°11	6°37	7°40
S 19	9 54 45	0✶3'36	11♒39	10°51	28°22	15°23	9°41	28° 1	15°16	24°11	29°13	6°27	7°37
M 20	9 58 41	1° 4'09	26°53	12°22	29°36	15°44	9°54	28° 8	15°17	24°14	29°15	6°17	7°33
T 21	10 2 38	2° 4'39	11✶59	13°53	0♈49	16° 5	10° 7	28°15	15°18	24°16	29°17	6° 7	7°30
W 22	10 6 34	3° 5'08	26°49	15°26	2° 3	16°27	10°20	28°23	15°20	24°18	29°18	5°59	7°27
T 23	10 10 31	4° 5'36	11♈14	17° 0	3°17	16°49	10°33	28°30	15°21	24°20	29°20	5°54	7°24
F 24	10 14 27	5° 6'01	25°11	18°35	4°31	17°11	10°46	28°37	15°23	24°22	29°22	5°52	7°21
S 25	10 18 24	6° 6'25	8♉39	20°10	5°44	17°33	10°59	28°44	15°25	24°24	29°23	5♌D51	7°17
S 26	10 22 20	7° 6'47	21°39	21°47	6°58	17°56	11°12	28°52	15°26	24°27	29°25	5°52	7°14
M 27	10 26 17	8° 7'07	4Ⅱ17	23°24	8°11	18°19	11°25	28°59	15°28	24°29	29°26	5♌R53	7°11
T 28	10 30 14	9✶7'25	16Ⅱ35	25♒ 3	9♈25	18Ⅱ43	11♈39	29♒ 6	15♉30	24✶31	29♑28	5♌53	7♌ 8

19

MARCH 2023 set for midnight GMT

Day	Sid.t	☉	☽	☿	♀	♂	♃	♄	♅	♆	♇	☊	Ω	⚸	⚷	Day
W 1	10 34 10	10♓ 7'41	28♊40	26♒43	10♈38	19♊ 7	11♈52	29♒13	15♉32	24♓33	29♑30	5°R50	7♉ 5	5♌46	13♈51	W 1
T 2	10 38 7	11° 7'54	10♋36	28°23	11°52	19°31	12° 6	29°20	15°34	24°35	29°31	5♉46	7° 2	5°53	13°54	T 2
F 3	10 42 3	12° 8'06	22°28	0♓ 5	13° 5	19°55	12°19	29°28	15°36	24°38	29°33	5°40	6°58	5°59	13°57	F 3
S 4	10 46 0	13° 8'16	4♌19	1°48	14°18	20°19	12°33	29°35	15°38	24°40	29°34	5°31	6°55	6° 6	14° 0	S 4
S 5	10 49 56	14° 8'24	16°12	3°31	15°31	20°44	12°46	29°42	15°40	24°42	29°36	5°21	6°52	6°13	14° 3	S 5
M 6	10 53 53	15° 8'30	28°11	5°16	16°44	21° 9	13° 0	29°49	15°42	24°44	29°37	5°11	6°49	6°19	14° 6	M 6
T 7	10 57 49	16° 8'34	10♍15	7° 2	17°58	21°35	13°14	29°56	15°44	24°47	29°39	5° 1	6°46	6°26	14°10	T 7
W 8	11 1 46	17° 8'36	22°27	8°49	19°10	22° 0	13°27	0♓ 3	15°46	24°49	29°40	4°53	6°43	6°33	14°13	W 8
T 9	11 5 43	18° 8'36	4♎47	10°37	20°23	22°26	13°41	0°10	15°48	24°51	29°42	4°47	6°39	6°40	14°16	T 9
F 10	11 9 39	19° 8'35	17°17	12°26	21°36	22°52	13°55	0°17	15°50	24°53	29°43	4°43	6°36	6°46	14°19	F 10
S 11	11 13 36	20° 8'31	29°57	14°17	22°49	23°18	14° 9	0°24	15°52	24°56	29°44	4°D42	6°33	6°53	14°23	S 11
S 12	11 17 32	21° 8'26	12♏50	16° 8	24° 2	23°45	14°23	0°31	15°55	24°58	29°46	4°42	6°30	7° 0	14°26	S 12
M13	11 21 29	22° 8'20	25°56	18° 1	25°14	24°11	14°37	0°38	15°57	25° 0	29°47	4°43	6°27	7° 6	14°29	M13
T 14	11 25 25	23° 8'12	9♐19	19°54	26°27	24°38	14°51	0°45	15°59	25° 2	29°49	4°45	6°23	7°13	14°32	T 14
W15	11 29 22	24° 8'02	22°59	21°49	27°39	25° 5	15° 5	0°52	16° 2	25° 5	29°50	4°R45	6°20	7°20	14°36	W15
T 16	11 33 18	25° 7'50	6♑59	23°45	28°52	25°32	15°19	0°59	16° 4	25° 7	29°51	4°45	6°17	7°27	14°39	T 16
F 17	11 37 15	26° 7'37	21°17	25°42	0♉ 4	26° 0	15°33	1° 6	16° 7	25° 9	29°52	4°42	6°14	7°33	14°43	F 17
S 18	11 41 12	27° 7'22	5♒51	27°40	1°17	26°27	15°47	1°12	16° 9	25°12	29°54	4°38	6°11	7°40	14°46	S 18
S 19	11 45 8	28° 7'06	20°36	29°38	2°29	26°55	16° 1	1°19	16°12	25°14	29°55	4°33	6° 8	7°47	14°49	S 19
M20	11 49 5	29° 6'47	5♓27	1♈38	3°41	27°23	16°15	1°26	16°14	25°16	29°56	4°28	6° 4	7°54	14°53	M20
T 21	11 53 1	0♈ 6'27	20°14	3°38	4°53	27°51	16°30	1°33	16°17	25°18	29°57	4°23	6° 1	8° 0	14°56	T 21
W22	11 56 58	1° 6'04	4♈49	5°38	6° 5	28°20	16°44	1°39	16°20	25°21	29°58	4°19	5°58	8° 7	15° 0	W22
T 23	12 0 54	2° 5'40	19° 7	7°39	7°17	28°48	16°58	1°46	16°22	25°23	29°59	4°16	5°55	8°14	15° 3	T 23
F 24	12 4 51	3° 5'13	3♉ 2	9°40	8°29	29°17	17°12	1°52	16°25	25°25	0♒ 1	4°D15	5°52	8°20	15° 7	F 24
S 25	12 8 47	4° 4'45	16°32	11°41	9°41	29°46	17°27	1°59	16°28	25°27	0° 2	4°16	5°49	8°27	15°10	S 25
S 26	12 12 44	5° 4'14	29°38	13°41	10°52	0♋15	17°41	2° 5	16°31	25°30	0° 3	4°17	5°45	8°34	15°13	S 26
M27	12 16 41	6° 3'41	12♊20	15°41	12° 4	0°44	17°55	2°12	16°33	25°32	0° 4	4°19	5°42	8°41	15°17	M27
T 28	12 20 37	7° 3'05	24°44	17°40	13°15	1°13	18°10	2°18	16°36	25°34	0° 5	4°20	5°39	8°47	15°20	T 28
W29	12 24 34	8° 2'28	6♋52	19°38	14°27	1°43	18°24	2°25	16°39	25°36	0° 6	4°R21	5°36	8°54	15°24	W29
T 30	12 28 30	9° 1'48	18°51	21°33	15°38	2°12	18°38	2°31	16°42	25°39	0° 7	4°20	5°33	9° 1	15°27	T 30
F 31	12 32 27	10♈ 1'06	0♌44	23♈27	16♉49	2♋42	18♈53	2♓37	16♉45	25♓41	0♒ 7	4♉19	5♉29	9♌ 7	15♈31	F 31

APRIL 2023 set for midnight GMT

Day	Sid.t	☉	☽	☿	♀	♂	♃	♄	♅	♆	♇	☊	☊	⚸	⚷	Day
S 1	12 36 23	11♈ 0'21	12♌36	25♈18	18♉ 1	3♋12	19♈ 7	2♓44	16♉48	25♓43	0♒ 8	4°R16	5♉26	9♌14	15♈35	S 1
S 2	12 40 20	11°59'34	24°31	27° 6	19°12	3°42	19°22	2°50	16°51	25°45	0° 9	4♉13	5°23	9°21	15°38	S 2
M 3	12 44 16	12°58'45	6♍33	28°51	20°22	4°12	19°36	2°56	16°54	25°48	0°10	4° 9	5°20	9°28	15°42	M 3
T 4	12 48 13	13°57'54	18°45	0♉32	21°33	4°42	19°51	3° 2	16°57	25°50	0°11	4° 6	5°17	9°34	15°45	T 4
W 5	12 52 9	14°57'00	1♎ 7	2° 9	22°44	5°13	20° 5	3° 8	17° 0	25°52	0°12	4° 3	5°14	9°41	15°49	W 5
T 6	12 56 6	15°56'04	13°42	3°41	23°55	5°43	20°19	3°14	17° 3	25°54	0°12	4° 1	5°10	9°48	15°52	T 6
F 7	13 0 3	16°55'07	26°30	5° 9	25° 5	6°14	20°34	3°20	17° 6	25°56	0°13	4° 0	5° 7	9°55	15°56	F 7
S 8	13 3 59	17°54'07	9♏32	6°32	26°16	6°45	20°48	3°26	17° 9	25°58	0°14	4°D 0	5° 4	10° 1	15°59	S 8
S 9	13 7 56	18°53'06	22°46	7°49	27°26	7°16	21° 3	3°32	17°12	26° 1	0°14	4° 1	5° 1	10° 8	16° 3	S 9
M10	13 11 52	19°52'02	6♐14	9° 1	28°36	7°47	21°17	3°37	17°15	26° 3	0°15	4° 2	4°58	10°15	16° 6	M10
T11	13 15 49	20°50'57	19°53	10° 8	29°46	8°18	21°32	3°43	17°19	26° 5	0°16	4° 3	4°54	10°21	16°10	T11
W12	13 19 45	21°49'51	3♑44	11° 8	0♊56	8°49	21°46	3°49	17°22	26° 7	0°16	4° 4	4°51	10°28	16°13	W12
T13	13 23 42	22°48'42	17°46	12° 3	2° 6	9°20	22° 1	3°54	17°25	26° 9	0°17	4°R 4	4°48	10°35	16°17	T13
F14	13 27 38	23°47'32	1♒57	12°51	3°16	9°52	22°15	4° 0	17°28	26°11	0°17	4° 4	4°45	10°42	16°20	F14
S15	13 31 35	24°46'20	16°16	13°34	4°25	10°23	22°30	4° 5	17°32	26°13	0°18	4° 4	4°42	10°48	16°24	S15
S16	13 35 32	25°45'07	0♓38	14°10	5°35	10°55	22°44	4°11	17°35	26°15	0°18	4° 3	4°39	10°55	16°27	S16
M17	13 39 28	26°43'51	15° 0	14°40	6°44	11°26	22°59	4°16	17°38	26°17	0°19	4° 2	4°35	11° 2	16°31	M17
T18	13 43 25	27°42'34	29°19	15° 3	7°53	11°58	23°13	4°22	17°41	26°19	0°19	4° 1	4°32	11° 9	16°34	T18
W19	13 47 21	28°41'15	13♈29	15°21	9° 2	12°30	23°28	4°27	17°45	26°21	0°20	4° 1	4°29	11°15	16°38	W19
T20	13 51 18	29°39'54	27°25	15°32	10°11	13° 2	23°42	4°32	17°48	26°23	0°20	4°D 1	4°26	11°22	16°41	T20
F21	13 55 14	0♉38'31	11♉ 5	15°R37	11°20	13°34	23°57	4°37	17°51	26°25	0°20	4° 1	4°23	11°29	16°45	F21
S22	13 59 11	1°37'07	24°26	15°36	12°29	14° 6	24°11	4°42	17°55	26°27	0°20	4° 1	4°20	11°35	16°48	S22
S23	14 3 7	2°35'40	7♊27	15°30	13°37	14°39	24°25	4°47	17°58	26°29	0°21	4° 1	4°16	11°42	16°52	S23
M24	14 7 4	3°34'11	20°10	15°18	14°46	15°11	24°40	4°52	18° 2	26°31	0°21	4°R 1	4°13	11°49	16°55	M24
T25	14 11 1	4°32'41	2♋35	15° 0	15°54	15°43	24°54	4°57	18° 5	26°33	0°21	4° 1	4°10	11°56	16°58	T25
W26	14 14 57	5°31'08	14°46	14°39	17° 2	16°16	25° 8	5° 2	18° 8	26°35	0°21	4° 1	4° 7	12° 2	17° 2	W26
T27	14 18 54	6°29'33	26°46	14°13	18°10	16°49	25°23	5° 6	18°12	26°37	0°22	4° 1	4° 4	12° 9	17° 5	T27
F28	14 22 50	7°27'56	8♌41	13°43	19°18	17°21	25°37	5°11	18°15	26°38	0°22	4°D 1	4° 0	12°16	17° 9	F28
S29	14 26 47	8°26'17	20°34	13°10	20°26	17°54	25°51	5°15	18°19	26°40	0°22	4° 1	3°57	12°22	17°12	S29
S30	14 30 43	9♉24'35	2♍30	12♉35	21♊33	18♋27	26♈ 6	5♓20	18♉22	26♓42	0♒22	4♉ 1	3♉54	12♌29	17♈15	S30

MAY 2023 set for midnight GMT

Day	Sid.t	☉	☽	☿	♀	♂	♃	♄	♅	♆	♇	☊	☊	⚸	⚷	Day
M 1	14 34 40	10♉22'52	14♍34	11°R57	22♊40	19♋ 0	26♈20	5♓24	18♉26	26♓44	0♒22	4♉ 2	3♉51	12♌36	17♈19	M 1
T 2	14 38 36	11°21'07	26°49	11♉19	23°48	19°33	26°34	5°29	18°29	26°46	0°R22	4° 2	3°48	12°43	17°22	T 2
W 3	14 42 33	12°19'19	9♎19	10°40	24°55	20° 6	26°48	5°33	18°32	26°47	0°22	4° 3	3°45	12°49	17°25	W 3
T 4	14 46 30	13°17'30	22° 6	10° 2	26° 1	20°39	27° 2	5°37	18°36	26°49	0°22	4° 4	3°41	12°56	17°28	T 4
F 5	14 50 26	14°15'39	5♏12	9°24	27° 8	21°12	27°17	5°41	18°39	26°51	0°22	4°R 4	3°38	13° 3	17°32	F 5
S 6	14 54 23	15°13'46	18°35	8°48	28°14	21°45	27°31	5°45	18°43	26°52	0°22	4° 4	3°35	13°10	17°35	S 6
S 7	14 58 19	16°11'52	2♐16	8°14	29°20	22°19	27°45	5°49	18°46	26°54	0°21	4° 3	3°32	13°16	17°38	S 7
M 8	15 2 16	17° 9'56	16°10	7°43	0♋26	22°52	27°59	5°53	18°50	26°56	0°21	4° 1	3°29	13°23	17°41	M 8
T 9	15 6 12	18° 7'59	0♑16	7°15	1°32	23°26	28°13	5°57	18°53	26°57	0°21	4° 0	3°26	13°30	17°44	T 9
W10	15 10 9	19° 6'00	14°29	6°50	2°38	23°59	28°27	6° 0	18°57	26°59	0°21	3°58	3°22	13°36	17°48	W10
T11	15 14 5	20° 4'00	28°45	6°30	3°43	24°33	28°41	6° 4	19° 0	27° 0	0°21	3°56	3°19	13°43	17°51	T11
F12	15 18 2	21° 1'58	13♒ 2	6°13	4°48	25° 6	28°55	6° 7	19° 4	27° 2	0°20	3°56	3°16	13°50	17°54	F12
S13	15 21 59	21°59'55	27°15	6° 1	5°53	25°40	29° 9	6°11	19° 7	27° 3	0°20	3°D55	3°13	13°57	17°57	S13
S14	15 25 55	22°57'51	11♓23	5°54	6°58	26°14	29°23	6°14	19°11	27° 5	0°20	3°56	3°10	14° 3	18° 0	S14
M15	15 29 52	23°55'46	25°24	5°D51	8° 2	26°48	29°36	6°17	19°14	27° 6	0°19	3°57	3° 6	14°10	18° 3	M15
T16	15 33 48	24°53'39	9♈16	5°53	9° 6	27°22	29°50	6°21	19°18	27° 8	0°19	3°59	3° 3	14°17	18° 6	T16
W17	15 37 45	25°51'31	22°58	5°59	10°10	27°56	0♉ 4	6°24	19°21	27° 9	0°19	4° 0	3° 0	14°23	18° 9	W17
T18	15 41 41	26°49'22	6♉28	6°10	11°14	28°30	0°17	6°27	19°25	27°11	0°18	4°R 0	2°57	14°30	18°12	T18
F19	15 45 38	27°47'12	19°45	6°25	12°17	29° 4	0°31	6°30	19°28	27°12	0°18	3°59	2°54	14°37	18°15	F19
S20	15 49 34	28°45'00	2♊49	6°45	13°21	29°38	0°45	6°32	19°31	27°13	0°17	3°57	2°51	14°44	18°17	S20
S21	15 53 31	29°42'47	15°38	7° 9	14°24	0♌12	0°58	6°35	19°35	27°14	0°17	3°54	2°47	14°50	18°20	S21
M22	15 57 28	0♊40'32	28°12	7°38	15°26	0°46	1°12	6°38	19°38	27°16	0°16	3°50	2°44	14°57	18°23	M22
T23	16 1 24	1°38'16	10♋33	8°10	16°28	1°21	1°25	6°40	19°42	27°17	0°16	3°45	2°41	15° 4	18°26	T23
W24	16 5 21	2°35'59	22°42	8°47	17°31	1°55	1°39	6°43	19°45	27°18	0°15	3°41	2°38	15°10	18°29	W24
T25	16 9 17	3°33'40	4♌42	9°27	18°32	2°29	1°52	6°45	19°49	27°19	0°14	3°37	2°35	15°17	18°31	T25
F26	16 13 14	4°31'19	16°36	10°11	19°34	3° 4	2° 5	6°47	19°52	27°21	0°14	3°34	2°32	15°24	18°34	F26
S27	16 17 10	5°28'57	28°28	10°59	20°35	3°38	2°18	6°49	19°55	27°22	0°13	3°33	2°28	15°31	18°37	S27
S28	16 21 7	6°26'34	10♍24	11°50	21°35	4°13	2°32	6°52	19°59	27°23	0°12	3°D32	2°25	15°37	18°39	S28
M29	16 25 4	7°24'09	22°27	12°45	22°36	4°48	2°45	6°53	20° 2	27°24	0°12	3°33	2°22	15°44	18°42	M29
T30	16 29 0	8°21'42	4♎42	13°43	23°36	5°22	2°58	6°55	20° 5	27°25	0°11	3°35	2°19	15°51	18°44	T30
W31	16 32 57	9♊19'14	17♎15	14♉45	24♋35	5♌57	3♉11	6♓57	20♉ 9	27♓26	0♒10	3♉37	2♉16	15♌58	18♈47	W31

JUNE 2023 set for midnight GMT

Day	Sid.t	☉	☽	☿	♀	♂	♃	♄	♅	♆	♇	☊	☊	⚸	⚷	Day
T 1	16 36 53	10♊16'45	0♏ 8	15♉49	25♋35	6♌32	3♉24	6♓59	20♉12	27♓27	0°R 9	3°R37	2♉12	16♌ 4	18♈49	T 1
F 2	16 40 50	11°14'15	13°24	16°57	26°33	7° 7	3°37	7° 0	20°15	27°28	0♒ 9	3♉37	2° 9	16°11	18°52	F 2
S 3	16 44 46	12°11'44	27° 4	18° 8	27°32	7°41	3°49	7° 2	20°19	27°29	0° 8	3°35	2° 6	16°18	18°54	S 3
S 4	16 48 43	13° 9'11	11♐ 7	19°21	28°30	8°16	4° 2	7° 3	20°22	27°30	0° 7	3°31	2° 3	16°24	18°57	S 4
M 5	16 52 39	14° 6'38	25°27	20°38	29°27	8°51	4°15	7° 5	20°25	27°30	0° 6	3°26	2° 0	16°31	18°59	M 5
T 6	16 56 36	15° 4'03	10♑ 1	21°58	0♌24	9°26	4°27	7° 6	20°28	27°31	0° 5	3°20	1°57	16°38	19° 1	T 6
W 7	17 0 33	16° 1'28	24°41	23°20	1°21	10° 1	4°40	7° 7	20°32	27°32	0° 4	3°14	1°53	16°45	19° 4	W 7
T 8	17 4 29	16°58'52	9♒20	24°46	2°17	10°36	4°53	7° 8	20°35	27°33	0° 3	3° 8	1°50	16°51	19° 6	T 8
F 9	17 8 26	17°56'16	23°52	26°14	3°13	11°12	5° 5	7° 9	20°38	27°33	0° 2	3° 4	1°47	16°58	19° 8	F 9
S 10	17 12 22	18°53'38	8♓12	27°45	4° 8	11°47	5°17	7°10	20°41	27°34	0° 1	3° 2	1°44	17° 5	19°10	S 10
S 11	17 16 19	19°51'01	22°17	29°18	5° 2	12°22	5°30	7°10	20°44	27°35	0° 0	3°D 2	1°41	17°11	19°12	S 11
M12	17 20 15	20°48'22	6♈ 7	0♊55	5°56	12°57	5°42	7°11	20°47	27°35	29♑59	3° 2	1°38	17°18	19°14	M12
T13	17 24 12	21°45'44	19°41	2°34	6°50	13°33	5°54	7°12	20°51	27°36	29°58	3° 3	1°34	17°25	19°16	T13
W14	17 28 8	22°43'05	3♉ 2	4°16	7°43	14° 8	6° 6	7°12	20°54	27°37	29°57	3°R 4	1°31	17°32	19°18	W14
T15	17 32 5	23°40'25	16° 9	6° 1	8°35	14°43	6°18	7°12	20°57	27°37	29°56	3° 3	1°28	17°38	19°20	T15
F 16	17 36 2	24°37'45	29° 4	7°48	9°26	15°19	6°30	7°12	21° 0	27°38	29°55	3° 0	1°25	17°45	19°22	F 16
S 17	17 39 58	25°35'05	11♊47	9°38	10°17	15°54	6°41	7°13	21° 3	27°38	29°54	2°55	1°22	17°52	19°24	S 17
S 18	17 43 55	26°32'24	24°20	11°30	11° 8	16°30	6°53	7°R13	21° 6	27°39	29°53	2°48	1°18	17°58	19°26	S 18
M19	17 47 51	27°29'42	6♋42	13°25	11°57	17° 5	7° 5	7°13	21° 9	27°39	29°52	2°38	1°15	18° 5	19°27	M19
T 20	17 51 48	28°27'00	18°54	15°22	12°46	17°41	7°16	7°12	21°12	27°39	29°51	2°28	1°12	18°12	19°29	T 20
W21	17 55 44	29°24'17	0♌58	17°22	13°34	18°17	7°28	7°12	21°15	27°40	29°49	2°18	1° 9	18°19	19°31	W21
T 22	17 59 41	0♋21'34	12°55	19°24	14°22	18°53	7°39	7°12	21°18	27°40	29°48	2° 8	1° 6	18°25	19°32	T 22
F 23	18 3 37	1°18'50	24°47	21°27	15° 8	19°28	7°50	7°11	21°20	27°40	29°47	2° 1	1° 3	18°32	19°34	F 23
S 24	18 7 34	2°16'05	6♍37	23°33	15°54	20° 4	8° 2	7°11	21°23	27°40	29°46	1°55	0°59	18°39	19°35	S 24
S 25	18 11 31	3°13'20	18°31	25°40	16°39	20°40	8°13	7°10	21°26	27°41	29°45	1°52	0°56	18°46	19°37	S 25
M26	18 15 27	4°10'34	0♎32	27°48	17°22	21°16	8°24	7° 9	21°29	27°41	29°43	1°D51	0°53	18°52	19°38	M26
T 27	18 19 24	5° 7'47	12°45	29°58	18° 5	21°52	8°34	7° 8	21°32	27°41	29°42	1°51	0°50	18°59	19°40	T 27
W28	18 23 20	6° 5'00	25°15	2♋ 8	18°47	22°28	8°45	7° 7	21°34	27°41	29°41	1°R52	0°47	19° 6	19°41	W28
T 29	18 27 17	7° 2'13	8♏ 8	4°19	19°28	23° 4	8°56	7° 6	21°37	27°41	29°40	1°52	0°44	19°12	19°42	T 29
F 30	18 31 13	7♋59'25	21♏27	6♋30	20♌ 8	23♌40	9♉ 6	7♓ 5	21♉40	27♓41	29♑38	1♉50	0♉40	19♌19	19♈43	F 30

JULY 2023 set for midnight GMT

Day	Sid.t	☉	☽	☿	♀	♂	♃	♄	♅	♆	♇	☊	☊	⚸	⚷	Day
S 1	18 35 10	8♋56'36	5♐14	8♋41	20♌47	24♌16	9♉17	7°R 4	21♉42	27°R41	29°R37	1°R46	0♉37	19♌26	19♈45	S 1
S 2	18 39 6	9°53'48	19°28	10°52	21°24	24°52	9°27	7♓ 3	21°45	27♓41	29♑36	1♉40	0°34	19°33	19°46	S 2
M 3	18 43 3	10°50'59	4♑ 6	13° 2	22° 0	25°28	9°38	7° 1	21°47	27°41	29°34	1°32	0°31	19°39	19°47	M 3
T 4	18 47 0	11°48'10	19° 1	15°11	22°36	26° 4	9°48	7° 0	21°50	27°41	29°33	1°22	0°28	19°46	19°48	T 4
W 5	18 50 56	12°45'21	4♒ 5	17°19	23° 9	26°41	9°58	6°58	21°52	27°41	29°32	1°12	0°24	19°53	19°49	W 5
T 6	18 54 53	13°42'32	19° 7	19°26	23°42	27°17	10° 8	6°56	21°55	27°41	29°30	1° 3	0°21	19°59	19°50	T 6
F 7	18 58 49	14°39'43	3♓58	21°32	24°13	27°53	10°17	6°55	21°57	27°41	29°29	0°56	0°18	20° 6	19°51	F 7
S 8	19 2 46	15°36'54	18°32	23°36	24°42	28°29	10°27	6°53	22° 0	27°40	29°28	0°51	0°15	20°13	19°51	S 8
S 9	19 6 42	16°34'06	2♈45	25°39	25°11	29° 6	10°37	6°51	22° 2	27°40	29°26	0°49	0°12	20°20	19°52	S 9
M10	19 10 39	17°31'18	16°34	27°40	25°37	29°42	10°46	6°49	22° 4	27°40	29°25	0°D48	0° 9	20°26	19°53	M10
T11	19 14 36	18°28'31	0♉ 3	29°39	26° 2	0♍19	10°56	6°46	22° 7	27°40	29°23	0°R48	0° 5	20°33	19°54	T11
W12	19 18 32	19°25'44	13°11	1♌37	26°25	0°55	11° 5	6°44	22° 9	27°39	29°22	0°48	0° 2	20°40	19°54	W12
T13	19 22 29	20°22'58	26° 4	3°33	26°47	1°32	11°14	6°42	22°11	27°39	29°21	0°46	29♈59	20°46	19°55	T13
F14	19 26 25	21°20'12	8♊42	5°26	27° 7	2° 8	11°23	6°39	22°13	27°38	29°19	0°41	29°56	20°53	19°55	F14
S15	19 30 22	22°17'26	21°10	7°18	27°25	2°45	11°32	6°37	22°15	27°38	29°18	0°34	29°53	21° 0	19°56	S15
S16	19 34 18	23°14'41	3♋27	9° 8	27°41	3°22	11°40	6°34	22°17	27°38	29°16	0°24	29°50	21° 7	19°56	S16
M17	19 38 15	24°11'57	15°37	10°57	27°55	3°58	11°49	6°32	22°19	27°37	29°15	0°11	29°46	21°13	19°57	M17
T18	19 42 11	25° 9'12	27°40	12°43	28° 7	4°35	11°57	6°29	22°21	27°37	29°13	29♈58	29°43	21°20	19°57	T18
W19	19 46 8	26° 6'29	9♌38	14°27	28°18	5°12	12° 6	6°26	22°23	27°36	29°12	29°44	29°40	21°27	19°57	W19
T20	19 50 5	27° 3'45	21°31	16°10	28°26	5°49	12°14	6°23	22°25	27°35	29°11	29°31	29°37	21°33	19°57	T20
F21	19 54 1	28° 1'02	3♍21	17°51	28°31	6°26	12°22	6°20	22°27	27°35	29° 9	29°20	29°34	21°40	19°58	F21
S22	19 57 58	28°58'19	15°11	19°29	28°35	7° 3	12°30	6°17	22°29	27°34	29° 8	29°12	29°30	21°47	19°58	S22
S23	20 1 54	29°55'36	27° 4	21° 6	28°R36	7°40	12°38	6°14	22°31	27°33	29° 6	29° 7	29°27	21°54	19°58	S23
M24	20 5 51	0♌52'54	9♎ 4	22°42	28°35	8°17	12°45	6°11	22°32	27°33	29° 5	29° 4	29°24	22° 0	19°R58	M24
T25	20 9 47	1°50'12	21°15	24°15	28°32	8°54	12°53	6° 8	22°34	27°32	29° 4	29° 3	29°21	22° 7	19°58	T25
W26	20 13 44	2°47'30	3♏42	25°46	28°26	9°31	13° 0	6° 4	22°36	27°31	29° 2	29° 3	29°18	22°14	19°58	W26
T27	20 17 40	3°44'49	16°32	27°16	28°18	10° 8	13° 7	6° 1	22°37	27°30	29° 1	29° 3	29°15	22°20	19°57	T27
F28	20 21 37	4°42'09	29°47	28°43	28° 7	10°45	13°14	5°57	22°39	27°30	28°59	29° 1	29°11	22°27	19°57	F28
S29	20 25 34	5°39'28	13♐31	0♍ 9	27°54	11°22	13°21	5°54	22°41	27°29	28°58	28°57	29° 8	22°34	19°57	S29
S30	20 29 30	6°36'49	27°44	1°32	27°39	11°59	13°28	5°50	22°42	27°28	28°56	28°51	29° 5	22°41	19°57	S30
M31	20 33 27	7♌34'10	12♑26	2♍54	27♌21	12♍37	13♉35	5♓46	22♉44	27♓27	28♑55	28♈42	29♈ 2	22♌47	19♈56	M31

AUGUST 2023 set for midnight GMT

Day	Sid.t	☉	☽	☿	♀	♂	♃	♄	♅	♆	♇	☊	☊	⚸	⚷	Day
T 1	20 37 23	8♌31'31	27♑29	4♍14	27°R 1	13♍14	13♉41	5°R43	22♉45	27°R26	28°R54	28°R32	28♈59	22♌54	19°R56	T 1
W 2	20 41 20	9°28'53	12♒45	5°31	26♌39	13°51	13°47	5♓39	22°46	27♓25	28♑52	28♈21	28°56	23° 1	19♈55	W 2
T 3	20 45 16	10°26'16	28° 2	6°47	26°15	14°29	13°53	5°35	22°48	27°24	28°51	28°12	28°52	23° 7	19°55	T 3
F 4	20 49 13	11°23'40	13♓10	8° 0	25°49	15° 6	13°59	5°31	22°49	27°23	28°49	28° 4	28°49	23°14	19°54	F 4
S 5	20 53 9	12°21'05	27°59	9°11	25°20	15°44	14° 5	5°27	22°50	27°22	28°48	27°59	28°46	23°21	19°54	S 5
S 6	20 57 6	13°18'31	12♈23	10°20	24°50	16°21	14°11	5°23	22°51	27°21	28°47	27°56	28°43	23°28	19°53	S 6
M 7	21 1 3	14°15'59	26°21	11°26	24°19	16°59	14°16	5°19	22°52	27°20	28°45	27°D55	28°40	23°34	19°52	M 7
T 8	21 4 59	15°13'28	9♉52	12°30	23°46	17°36	14°21	5°15	22°53	27°19	28°44	27°R55	28°36	23°41	19°52	T 8
W 9	21 8 56	16°10'58	23° 0	13°31	23°11	18°14	14°26	5°11	22°54	27°18	28°43	27°55	28°33	23°48	19°51	W 9
T 10	21 12 52	17° 8'29	5♊47	14°30	22°36	18°52	14°31	5° 7	22°55	27°17	28°41	27°54	28°30	23°54	19°50	T 10
F 11	21 16 49	18° 6'02	18°17	15°25	22° 0	19°29	14°36	5° 3	22°56	27°15	28°40	27°50	28°27	24° 1	19°49	F 11
S 12	21 20 45	19° 3'36	0♋35	16°18	21°23	20° 7	14°41	4°58	22°57	27°14	28°39	27°44	28°24	24° 8	19°48	S 12
S 13	21 24 42	20° 1'12	12°42	17° 8	20°46	20°45	14°45	4°54	22°58	27°13	28°37	27°35	28°21	24°14	19°47	S 13
M14	21 28 38	20°58'49	24°43	17°54	20° 8	21°23	14°49	4°50	22°59	27°12	28°36	27°24	28°17	24°21	19°46	M14
T 15	21 32 35	21°56'27	6♌39	18°37	19°31	22° 1	14°53	4°45	23° 0	27°10	28°35	27°12	28°14	24°28	19°45	T 15
W16	21 36 32	22°54'06	18°32	19°16	18°54	22°39	14°57	4°41	23° 0	27° 9	28°33	27° 0	28°11	24°35	19°44	W16
T 17	21 40 28	23°51'47	0♍23	19°51	18°18	23°17	15° 1	4°37	23° 1	27° 8	28°32	26°49	28° 8	24°41	19°42	T 17
F 18	21 44 25	24°49'29	12°13	20°22	17°43	23°55	15° 5	4°32	23° 1	27° 7	28°31	26°39	28° 5	24°48	19°41	F 18
S 19	21 48 21	25°47'12	24° 6	20°49	17° 8	24°33	15° 8	4°28	23° 2	27° 5	28°30	26°32	28° 2	24°55	19°40	S 19
S 20	21 52 18	26°44'56	6♎ 2	21°12	16°35	25°11	15°11	4°23	23° 2	27° 4	28°28	26°28	27°58	25° 1	19°39	S 20
M21	21 56 14	27°42'42	18° 6	21°29	16° 3	25°49	15°14	4°19	23° 3	27° 2	28°27	26°25	27°55	25° 8	19°37	M21
T 22	22 0 11	28°40'28	0♏19	21°42	15°33	26°27	15°17	4°14	23° 3	27° 1	28°26	26°D25	27°52	25°15	19°36	T 22
W23	22 4 7	29°38'16	12°48	21°49	15° 4	27° 5	15°19	4°10	23° 4	27° 0	28°25	26°26	27°49	25°22	19°34	W23
T 24	22 8 4	0♍36'05	25°35	21°R51	14°38	27°44	15°22	4° 5	23° 4	26°58	28°24	26°R27	27°46	25°28	19°33	T 24
F 25	22 12 1	1°33'55	8♐46	21°47	14°13	28°22	15°24	4° 1	23° 4	26°57	28°23	26°27	27°42	25°35	19°31	F 25
S 26	22 15 57	2°31'47	22°23	21°38	13°50	29° 0	15°26	3°56	23° 4	26°55	28°21	26°25	27°39	25°42	19°30	S 26
S 27	22 19 54	3°29'40	6♑28	21°22	13°30	29°39	15°28	3°52	23° 4	26°54	28°20	26°21	27°36	25°48	19°28	S 27
M28	22 23 50	4°27'34	21° 0	21° 0	13°12	0♎17	15°29	3°47	23° 4	26°52	28°19	26°15	27°33	25°55	19°26	M28
T 29	22 27 47	5°25'29	5♒56	20°33	12°56	0°56	15°31	3°43	23°R 5	26°51	28°18	26° 8	27°30	26° 2	19°24	T 29
W30	22 31 43	6°23'25	21° 7	20° 0	12°43	1°34	15°32	3°38	23° 4	26°49	28°17	26° 1	27°27	26° 9	19°23	W30
T 31	22 35 40	7♍21'23	6♓24	19♍21	12♌32	2♎13	15♉33	3♓34	23♉ 4	26♓48	28♑16	25♈54	27♈23	26♌15	19♈21	T 31

SEPTEMBER 2023 set for midnight GMT

Day	Sid.t	☉	☽	☿	♀	♂	♃	♄	♅	♆	♇	☊	☊	⚸	⚷	Day
F 1	22 39 36	8♍19'23	21♓36	18°R37	12°R23	2♎51	15♉34	3°R29	23°R 4	26°R46	28°R15	25°R48	27♈20	26♌22	19°R19	F 1
S 2	22 43 33	9°17'24	6♈33	17♍48	12♌17	3°30	15°34	3♓25	23♉ 4	26♓45	28♑14	25♈45	27°17	26°29	19♈17	S 2
S 3	22 47 30	10°15'27	21° 7	16°55	12°14	4° 9	15°35	3°20	23° 4	26°43	28°13	25°D43	27°14	26°35	19°15	S 3
M 4	22 51 26	11°13'32	5♉15	16° 0	12°D12	4°47	15°35	3°16	23° 4	26°42	28°12	25°44	27°11	26°42	19°13	M 4
T 5	22 55 23	12°11'39	18°54	15° 2	12°13	5°26	15°R35	3°11	23° 3	26°40	28°11	25°45	27° 7	26°49	19°11	T 5
W 6	22 59 19	13° 9'48	2♊ 7	14° 4	12°17	6° 5	15°35	3° 7	23° 3	26°38	28°10	25°46	27° 4	26°55	19° 9	W 6
T 7	23 3 16	14° 7'59	14°56	13° 6	12°22	6°44	15°34	3° 2	23° 3	26°37	28° 9	25°R47	27° 1	27° 2	19° 7	T 7
F 8	23 7 12	15° 6'12	27°26	12°10	12°30	7°23	15°34	2°58	23° 2	26°35	28° 8	25°46	26°58	27° 9	19° 5	F 8
S 9	23 11 9	16° 4'27	9♋41	11°16	12°40	8° 2	15°33	2°53	23° 2	26°34	28° 8	25°43	26°55	27°16	19° 3	S 9
S 10	23 15 5	17° 2'44	21°44	10°27	12°52	8°41	15°32	2°49	23° 1	26°32	28° 7	25°39	26°52	27°22	19° 1	S 10
M11	23 19 2	18° 1'03	3♌40	9°44	13° 7	9°20	15°31	2°45	23° 0	26°30	28° 6	25°33	26°48	27°29	18°58	M11
T 12	23 22 59	18°59'24	15°32	9° 7	13°23	9°59	15°29	2°40	23° 0	26°29	28° 5	25°27	26°45	27°36	18°56	T 12
W13	23 26 55	19°57'47	27°23	8°37	13°41	10°38	15°28	2°36	22°59	26°27	28° 4	25°20	26°42	27°42	18°54	W13
T 14	23 30 52	20°56'12	9♍15	8°16	14° 1	11°17	15°26	2°32	22°58	26°25	28° 4	25°14	26°39	27°49	18°51	T 14
F 15	23 34 48	21°54'39	21° 9	8° 4	14°23	11°56	15°24	2°28	22°57	26°24	28° 3	25° 8	26°36	27°56	18°49	F 15
S 16	23 38 45	22°53'07	3♎ 8	8°D 0	14°47	12°36	15°22	2°24	22°57	26°22	28° 2	25° 5	26°33	28° 2	18°47	S 16
S 17	23 42 41	23°51'37	15°13	8° 6	15°12	13°15	15°19	2°20	22°56	26°20	28° 2	25° 3	26°29	28° 9	18°44	S 17
M18	23 46 38	24°50'10	27°27	8°22	15°39	13°54	15°17	2°16	22°55	26°19	28° 1	25°D 2	26°26	28°16	18°42	M18
T 19	23 50 34	25°48'44	9♏51	8°47	16° 8	14°34	15°14	2°12	22°54	26°17	28° 0	25° 3	26°23	28°23	18°39	T 19
W20	23 54 31	26°47'19	22°28	9°21	16°38	15°13	15°11	2° 8	22°53	26°15	28° 0	25° 5	26°20	28°29	18°37	W20
T 21	23 58 28	27°45'57	5♐21	10° 4	17° 9	15°53	15° 8	2° 4	22°52	26°14	27°59	25° 6	26°17	28°36	18°35	T 21
F 22	0 2 24	28°44'36	18°33	10°55	17°42	16°32	15° 5	2° 0	22°50	26°12	27°59	25° 8	26°13	28°43	18°32	F 22
S 23	0 6 21	29°43'17	2♑ 5	11°54	18°16	17°12	15° 1	1°56	22°49	26°10	27°58	25°R 8	26°10	28°49	18°29	S 23
S 24	0 10 17	0♎42'00	16° 1	13° 0	18°52	17°52	14°57	1°53	22°48	26° 9	27°58	25° 7	26° 7	28°56	18°27	S 24
M25	0 14 14	1°40'44	0♒18	14°12	19°29	18°31	14°53	1°49	22°47	26° 7	27°57	25° 5	26° 4	29° 3	18°24	M25
T 26	0 18 10	2°39'30	14°56	15°31	20° 7	19°11	14°49	1°45	22°45	26° 6	27°57	25° 3	26° 1	29° 9	18°22	T 26
W27	0 22 7	3°38'18	29°49	16°54	20°46	19°51	14°45	1°42	22°44	26° 4	27°56	25° 0	25°58	29°16	18°19	W27
T 28	0 26 3	4°37'07	14♓49	18°22	21°27	20°31	14°40	1°38	22°43	26° 2	27°56	24°57	25°54	29°23	18°17	T 28
F 29	0 30 0	5°35'58	29°49	19°54	22° 9	21°10	14°36	1°35	22°41	26° 1	27°56	24°55	25°51	29°30	18°14	F 29
S 30	0 33 56	6♎34'51	14♈40	21♍30	22♌51	21♎50	14♉31	1♓32	22♉40	25♓59	27♑55	24♈54	25♈48	29♌36	18♈11	S 30

OCTOBER 2023 set for midnight GMT

Day	Sid.t	☉	☽	☿	♀	♂	♃	♄	♅	♆	♇	☊	☊	⚸	⚷	Day
S 1	0 37 53	7♎33'47	29♈13	23♍ 8	23♌35	22♎30	14°R26	1°R29	22°R38	25°R57	27°R55	24°D54	25♈45	29♌43	18°R 9	S 1
M 2	0 41 50	8°32'44	13♉24	24°48	24°20	23°10	14♉21	1♓25	22♉37	25♓56	27♑55	24♈54	25°42	29°50	18♈ 6	M 2
T 3	0 45 46	9°31'44	27°10	26°31	25° 5	23°50	14°16	1°22	22°35	25°54	27°54	24°55	25°39	29°56	18° 3	T 3
W 4	0 49 43	10°30'46	10♊29	28°15	25°52	24°30	14°10	1°19	22°34	25°53	27°54	24°57	25°35	0♍ 3	18° 1	W 4
T 5	0 53 39	11°29'50	23°24	29°59	26°39	25°11	14° 4	1°16	22°32	25°51	27°54	24°58	25°32	0°10	17°58	T 5
F 6	0 57 36	12°28'57	5♋58	1♎45	27°28	25°51	13°59	1°14	22°30	25°49	27°54	24°58	25°29	0°16	17°55	F 6
S 7	1 1 32	13°28'06	18°14	3°31	28°17	26°31	13°53	1°11	22°28	25°48	27°54	24°R58	25°26	0°23	17°52	S 7
S 8	1 5 29	14°27'17	0♌18	5°17	29° 7	27°11	13°47	1° 8	22°27	25°46	27°54	24°58	25°23	0°30	17°50	S 8
M 9	1 9 26	15°26'31	12°13	7° 4	29°57	27°52	13°40	1° 5	22°25	25°45	27°54	24°57	25°19	0°37	17°47	M 9
T 10	1 13 22	16°25'46	24° 4	8°50	0♍49	28°32	13°34	1° 3	22°23	25°43	27°54	24°56	25°16	0°43	17°44	T 10
W11	1 17 19	17°25'04	5♍55	10°36	1°41	29°13	13°28	1° 1	22°21	25°42	27°D54	24°55	25°13	0°50	17°41	W11
T 12	1 21 15	18°24'24	17°49	12°22	2°34	29°53	13°21	0°58	22°19	25°40	27°54	24°54	25°10	0°57	17°39	T 12
F 13	1 25 12	19°23'47	29°49	14° 8	3°28	0♏34	13°14	0°56	22°17	25°39	27°54	24°53	25° 7	1° 3	17°36	F 13
S 14	1 29 8	20°23'11	11♎57	15°53	4°22	1°14	13° 7	0°54	22°15	25°37	27°54	24°53	25° 4	1°10	17°33	S 14
S 15	1 33 5	21°22'38	24°16	17°37	5°17	1°55	13° 0	0°52	22°13	25°36	27°54	24°D52	25° 0	1°17	17°31	S 15
M16	1 37 1	22°22'06	6♏45	19°21	6°12	2°36	12°53	0°50	22°11	25°34	27°54	24°53	24°57	1°23	17°28	M16
T 17	1 40 58	23°21'37	19°28	21° 4	7° 8	3°16	12°46	0°48	22° 9	25°33	27°54	24°53	24°54	1°30	17°25	T 17
W18	1 44 54	24°21'10	2♐23	22°47	8° 4	3°57	12°39	0°46	22° 7	25°31	27°54	24°53	24°51	1°37	17°22	W18
T 19	1 48 51	25°20'44	15°32	24°29	9° 1	4°38	12°31	0°44	22° 5	25°30	27°54	24°R53	24°48	1°44	17°20	T 19
F 20	1 52 48	26°20'20	28°55	26°11	9°59	5°19	12°24	0°43	22° 3	25°29	27°55	24°53	24°45	1°50	17°17	F 20
S 21	1 56 44	27°19'58	12♑33	27°51	10°57	6° 0	12°16	0°41	22° 1	25°27	27°55	24°53	24°41	1°57	17°14	S 21
S 22	2 0 41	28°19'38	26°26	29°32	11°56	6°41	12° 8	0°40	21°58	25°26	27°55	24°D52	24°38	2° 4	17°12	S 22
M23	2 4 37	29°19'20	10♒33	1♏11	12°55	7°22	12° 1	0°39	21°56	25°25	27°56	24°53	24°35	2°10	17° 9	M23
T 24	2 8 34	0♏19'03	24°52	2°50	13°54	8° 3	11°53	0°37	21°54	25°23	27°56	24°53	24°32	2°17	17° 6	T 24
W25	2 12 30	1°18'47	9♓20	4°29	14°54	8°44	11°45	0°36	21°52	25°22	27°56	24°53	24°29	2°24	17° 4	W25
T 26	2 16 27	2°18'34	23°54	6° 6	15°55	9°25	11°37	0°35	21°49	25°21	27°57	24°54	24°25	2°30	17° 1	T 26
F 27	2 20 23	3°18'22	8♈29	7°44	16°55	10° 7	11°29	0°34	21°47	25°20	27°57	24°55	24°22	2°37	16°59	F 27
S 28	2 24 20	4°18'12	22°58	9°20	17°57	10°48	11°21	0°34	21°45	25°18	27°58	24°R55	24°19	2°44	16°56	S 28
S 29	2 28 17	5°18'03	7♉17	10°57	18°58	11°29	11°13	0°33	21°42	25°17	27°58	24°55	24°16	2°50	16°53	S 29
M30	2 32 13	6°17'57	21°19	12°32	20° 0	12°11	11° 5	0°32	21°40	25°16	27°59	24°54	24°13	2°57	16°51	M30
T 31	2 36 10	7♏17'53	5♊ 1	14♏ 8	21♍ 3	12♏52	10♉57	0♓32	21♉38	25♓15	27♑59	24♈52	24♈10	3♍ 4	16♈48	T 31

NOVEMBER 2023 set for midnight GMT

Day	Sid.t	☉	☽	☿	♀	♂	♃	♄	♅	♆	♇	☊	☊	⚸	⚷	Day
W 1	2 40 6	8♏17'51	18♊22	15♏42	22♍ 5	13♏34	10°R49	0°R31	21°R35	25°R14	28♑ 0	24°R51	24♈ 6	3♍11	16°R46	W 1
T 2	2 44 3	9°17'51	1♋20	17°17	23° 9	14°15	10♉40	0♓31	21♉33	25♓13	28° 1	24♈49	24° 3	3°17	16♈43	T 2
F 3	2 47 59	10°17'53	13°57	18°50	24°12	14°57	10°32	0°31	21°30	25°12	28° 1	24°47	24° 0	3°24	16°41	F 3
S 4	2 51 56	11°17'58	26°17	20°24	25°16	15°38	10°24	0°D31	21°28	25°11	28° 2	24°45	23°57	3°31	16°38	S 4
S 5	2 55 52	12°18'04	8♌22	21°57	26°20	16°20	10°16	0°31	21°25	25°10	28° 3	24°D45	23°54	3°37	16°36	S 5
M 6	2 59 49	13°18'12	20°18	23°29	27°24	17° 2	10° 8	0°31	21°23	25° 9	28° 3	24°45	23°50	3°44	16°34	M 6
T 7	3 3 46	14°18'23	2♍ 9	25° 1	28°29	17°44	10° 0	0°31	21°20	25° 8	28° 4	24°46	23°47	3°51	16°31	T 7
W 8	3 7 42	15°18'35	14° 0	26°33	29°34	18°25	9°52	0°32	21°18	25° 7	28° 5	24°47	23°44	3°57	16°29	W 8
T 9	3 11 39	16°18'49	25°56	28° 5	0♎39	19° 7	9°43	0°32	21°16	25° 6	28° 6	24°49	23°41	4° 4	16°27	T 9
F 10	3 15 35	17°19'06	8♎ 0	29°36	1°45	19°49	9°35	0°33	21°13	25° 5	28° 7	24°50	23°38	4°11	16°24	F 10
S 11	3 19 32	18°19'24	20°17	1♐ 6	2°51	20°31	9°27	0°33	21°11	25° 4	28° 7	24°R51	23°35	4°17	16°22	S 11
S 12	3 23 28	19°19'44	2♏49	2°37	3°57	21°13	9°20	0°34	21° 8	25° 3	28° 8	24°51	23°31	4°24	16°20	S 12
M13	3 27 25	20°20'06	15°37	4° 7	5° 3	21°55	9°12	0°35	21° 6	25° 3	28° 9	24°50	23°28	4°31	16°18	M13
T 14	3 31 21	21°20'30	28°41	5°36	6°10	22°38	9° 4	0°36	21° 3	25° 2	28°10	24°47	23°25	4°38	16°16	T 14
W15	3 35 18	22°20'56	12♐ 2	7° 5	7°17	23°20	8°56	0°37	21° 1	25° 1	28°11	24°43	23°22	4°44	16°14	W15
T 16	3 39 15	23°21'23	25°36	8°34	8°24	24° 2	8°48	0°38	20°58	25° 0	28°12	24°38	23°19	4°51	16°12	T 16
F 17	3 43 11	24°21'51	9♑23	10° 2	9°31	24°44	8°41	0°39	20°56	25° 0	28°13	24°34	23°16	4°58	16°10	F 17
S 18	3 47 8	25°22'21	23°19	11°30	10°39	25°27	8°33	0°41	20°53	24°59	28°14	24°30	23°12	5° 4	16° 8	S 18
S 19	3 51 4	26°22'52	7♒21	12°58	11°47	26° 9	8°26	0°42	20°51	24°58	28°15	24°27	23° 9	5°11	16° 6	S 19
M20	3 55 1	27°23'24	21°28	14°24	12°55	26°51	8°19	0°44	20°48	24°58	28°16	24°D26	23° 6	5°18	16° 4	M20
T 21	3 58 57	28°23'58	5♓37	15°50	14° 3	27°34	8°11	0°45	20°46	24°57	28°18	24°26	23° 3	5°24	16° 2	T 21
W22	4 2 54	29°24'33	19°47	17°16	15°11	28°17	8° 4	0°47	20°43	24°57	28°19	24°27	23° 0	5°31	16° 0	W22
T 23	4 6 50	0♐25'08	3♈56	18°41	16°20	28°59	7°57	0°49	20°41	24°56	28°20	24°28	22°56	5°38	15°58	T 23
F 24	4 10 47	1°25'45	18° 2	20° 5	17°28	29°42	7°51	0°51	20°38	24°56	28°21	24°R29	22°53	5°44	15°57	F 24
S 25	4 14 44	2°26'23	2♉ 3	21°28	18°37	0♐24	7°44	0°53	20°36	24°56	28°22	24°29	22°50	5°51	15°55	S 25
S 26	4 18 40	3°27'03	15°56	22°49	19°46	1° 7	7°37	0°55	20°33	24°55	28°24	24°27	22°47	5°58	15°53	S 26
M27	4 22 37	4°27'43	29°37	24°10	20°55	1°50	7°31	0°58	20°31	24°55	28°25	24°23	22°44	6° 4	15°52	M27
T 28	4 26 33	5°28'26	13♊ 5	25°29	22° 5	2°33	7°24	1° 0	20°29	24°55	28°26	24°18	22°41	6°11	15°50	T 28
W29	4 30 30	6°29'09	26°16	26°47	23°14	3°16	7°18	1° 2	20°26	24°54	28°28	24°10	22°37	6°18	15°49	W29
T 30	4 34 26	7♐29'54	9♋ 9	28♐ 3	24♎24	3♐59	7♉12	1♓ 5	20♉24	24♓54	28♑29	24♈ 2	22♈34	6♍25	15♈47	T 30

DECEMBER 2023 set for midnight GMT

Day	Sid.t	☉	☽	☿	♀	♂	♃	♄	♅	♆	♇	☋	☊	⚸	⚷	Day
F 1	4 38 23	8♐30'40	21♋45	29♐17	25♎34	4♐42	7°R 6	1♓ 8	20°R22	24°R54	28♑30	23°R55	22♈31	6♍31	15°R46	F 1
S 2	4 42 20	9°31'28	4♌ 5	0♑28	26°44	5°25	7♉ 1	1°11	20♉19	24♓54	28°32	23♈48	22°28	6°38	15♈44	S 2
S 3	4 46 16	10°32'17	16°10	1°36	27°54	6° 8	6°55	1°13	20°17	24°54	28°33	23°43	22°25	6°45	15°43	S 3
M 4	4 50 13	11°33'07	28° 6	2°42	29° 5	6°51	6°50	1°16	20°15	24°53	28°34	23°39	22°22	6°51	15°42	M 4
T 5	4 54 9	12°33'58	9♍57	3°44	0♏15	7°34	6°44	1°19	20°12	24°53	28°36	23°D38	22°18	6°58	15°41	T 5
W 6	4 58 6	13°34'51	21°47	4°41	1°26	8°17	6°39	1°23	20°10	24°53	28°37	23°38	22°15	7° 5	15°39	W 6
T 7	5 2 2	14°35'46	3♎42	5°34	2°36	9° 1	6°34	1°26	20° 8	24°D53	28°39	23°40	22°12	7°11	15°38	T 7
F 8	5 5 59	15°36'41	15°48	6°21	3°47	9°44	6°30	1°29	20° 6	24°53	28°40	23°41	22° 9	7°18	15°37	F 8
S 9	5 9 55	16°37'38	28° 8	7° 2	4°58	10°27	6°25	1°33	20° 4	24°53	28°42	23°R41	22° 6	7°25	15°36	S 9
S 10	5 13 52	17°38'36	10♏47	7°37	6° 9	11°11	6°21	1°36	20° 1	24°54	28°43	23°39	22° 2	7°31	15°35	S 10
M11	5 17 49	18°39'35	23°48	8° 3	7°21	11°54	6°17	1°40	19°59	24°54	28°45	23°35	21°59	7°38	15°34	M11
T 12	5 21 45	19°40'35	7♐12	8°21	8°32	12°38	6°13	1°43	19°57	24°54	28°47	23°29	21°56	7°45	15°33	T 12
W13	5 25 42	20°41'37	20°57	8°R29	9°43	13°21	6° 9	1°47	19°55	24°54	28°48	23°20	21°53	7°51	15°33	W13
T 14	5 29 38	21°42'39	4♑59	8°27	10°55	14° 5	6° 5	1°51	19°53	24°54	28°50	23°10	21°50	7°58	15°32	T 14
F 15	5 33 35	22°43'42	19°15	8°14	12° 7	14°49	6° 2	1°55	19°51	24°55	28°51	23° 0	21°47	8° 5	15°31	F 15
S 16	5 37 31	23°44'45	3♒39	7°49	13°18	15°33	5°59	1°59	19°49	24°55	28°53	22°51	21°43	8°11	15°31	S 16
S 17	5 41 28	24°45'49	18° 3	7°13	14°30	16°16	5°56	2° 3	19°47	24°55	28°55	22°44	21°40	8°18	15°30	S 17
M18	5 45 24	25°46'53	2♓24	6°25	15°42	17° 0	5°53	2° 7	19°45	24°56	28°56	22°39	21°37	8°25	15°29	M18
T 19	5 49 21	26°47'57	16°38	5°27	16°54	17°44	5°50	2°12	19°44	24°56	28°58	22°37	21°34	8°32	15°29	T 19
W20	5 53 18	27°49'02	0♈43	4°19	18° 6	18°28	5°48	2°16	19°42	24°56	29° 0	22°D36	21°31	8°38	15°29	W20
T 21	5 57 14	28°50'07	14°38	3° 4	19°18	19°12	5°45	2°21	19°40	24°57	29° 2	22°37	21°28	8°45	15°28	T 21
F 22	6 1 11	29°51'12	28°23	1°44	20°30	19°56	5°43	2°25	19°38	24°57	29° 3	22°R37	21°24	8°52	15°28	F 22
S 23	6 5 7	0♑52'18	11♉59	0°22	21°43	20°40	5°42	2°30	19°37	24°58	29° 5	22°35	21°21	8°58	15°28	S 23
S 24	6 9 4	1°53'23	25°25	28♐59	22°55	21°24	5°40	2°34	19°35	24°59	29° 7	22°31	21°18	9° 5	15°27	S 24
M25	6 13 0	2°54'30	8♊42	27°40	24° 8	22° 8	5°39	2°39	19°33	24°59	29° 9	22°24	21°15	9°12	15°27	M25
T 26	6 16 57	3°55'36	21°47	26°27	25°20	22°52	5°38	2°44	19°32	25° 0	29°10	22°14	21°12	9°18	15°27	T 26
W27	6 20 53	4°56'43	4♋40	25°20	26°33	23°37	5°37	2°49	19°30	25° 1	29°12	22° 2	21° 8	9°25	15°D27	W27
T 28	6 24 50	5°57'50	17°21	24°23	27°45	24°21	5°36	2°54	19°29	25° 1	29°14	21°48	21° 5	9°32	15°27	T 28
F 29	6 28 47	6°58'57	29°48	23°36	28°58	25° 5	5°35	2°59	19°27	25° 2	29°16	21°35	21° 2	9°38	15°27	F 29
S 30	6 32 43	8° 0'04	12♌ 2	22°59	0♐11	25°50	5°35	3° 4	19°26	25° 3	29°18	21°22	20°59	9°45	15°27	S 30
S 31	6 36 40	9♑ 1'12	24♌ 5	22♐33	1♐24	26♐34	5°D35	3♓ 9	19♉24	25♓ 4	29♑20	21♈12	20♈56	9♍52	15♈28	S 31

MOON PHASES 2023

All times are GMT

January

				Moon in
Full Moon	6th	23.08	16°22	Capricorn
Last Quarter	15th	02.10	24°38	Libra
New Moon	21st	20.53	01°33	Aquarius
First Quarter	28th	15.19	08°26	Taurus

February

Full Moon	5th	18.29	16°41	Leo
Last Quarter	13th	16.01	24°40	Scorpio
New Moon	20th	07.06	01°22	Pisces
First Quarter	27th	08.06	08°27	Gemini

March

Full Moon	7th	12.40	16°40	Virgo
Last Quarter	15th	02.08	24°13	Sagittarius
New Moon	21st	17.23	00°50	Aries
First Quarter	29th	02.32	08°09	Cancer

April

Full Moon	6th	04.34	16°07	Libra
Last Quarter	13th	09.11	23°11	Capricorn
New Moon	20th	04.12	29°50	Aries
First Quarter	27th	21.20	07°21	Leo

May

Full Moon	5th	17.34	14°58	Scorpio
Last Quarter	12th	14.28	21°37	Aquarius
New Moon	19th	15.53	28°25	Taurus
First Quarter	27th	15.22	06°06	Virgo

June

Full Moon	4th	03.42	13°18	Sagittarius
Last Quarter	10th	19.31	19°40	Pisces
New Moon	18th	04.37	26°43	Gemini
First Quarter	26th	07.50	04°29	Libra

July

			Moon in
Full Moon	3rd	11.39	11°19 Capricorn
Last Quarter	10th	01.48	17°36 Aries
New Moon	17th	18.32	24°56 Cancer
First Quarter	25th	22.07	02°43 Scorpio

August

Full Moon	1st	18.32	09°16 Aquarius
Last Quarter	8th	10.28	15°39 Taurus
New Moon	16th	09.38	23°17 Leo
First Quarter	24th	09.57	01°00 Sagittarius
Full Moon	31st	01.36	07°25 Pisces

September

Last Quarter	6th	22.21	14°04 Gemini
New Moon	15th	01.40	21°59 Virgo
First Quarter	22nd	19.32	29°32 Sagittarius
Full Moon	29th	09.57	06°00 Aries

October

Last Quarter	6th	13.48	13°03 Cancer
New Moon	14th	17.55	21°08 Libra
First Quarter	22nd	03.29	28°28 Capricorn
Full Moon	28th	20.24	05°09 Taurus

November

Last Quarter	5th	08.37	12°40 Leo
New Moon	13th	09.27	20°44 Scorpio
First Quarter	20th	10.50	27°51 Aquarius
Full Moon	27th	09.16	04°51 Gemini

December

Last Quarter	5th	05.49	12°49 Virgo
New Moon	12th	23.32	20°40 Sagittarius
First Quarter	19th	18.39	27°35 Pisces
Full Moon	27th	00.33	04°58 Cancer

All times are GMT

THE VOID-OF-COURSE MOON

Astrologically, the Moon is regarded as being Void-of-Course after she has made her last aspect to any planet and before she enters a new sign.

What does this mean in practice? Well, the Moon sets the emotional 'tone' of the day according to what sign she is in and which planets she is aspecting. She makes aspects to every one of the planets as she travels through each sign, going through all the combinations of tone possible in that sign. The tone of each day is always different.

As an example, take the very different effects of a Moon-Mercury trine in different signs: the Moon in Leo trining Mercury in Sagittarius and the Moon in Virgo trining Mercury in Capricorn. The first would produce dramatic, dynamic results in the areas of travel and communication - a speed record might be broken, or a new car design introduced. The second aspect would have the less spectacular (but no less important!) effect of improving efficiency and workrate in some area of public transport or mass telecommunications.

When the Moon has made her final planetary aspect in a sign, there is no more for her to say, so to speak. Everything has been done, the time is 'empty' and she has no more partners to dance with until she enters a new sign and begins all over again with a new costume. Until then, she is Void-of-Course.

We are all sensitive to the Moon to some degree, so during this Void time we may feel vacant, apathetic and without guidance. Our judgement is poor, our reactions awry. Plans and actions initiated during this time are unlikely to amount to anything. They won't lead to disaster - they simply won't get anywhere and may just fizzle out. So, during this time it would be advisable not to try anything new or start anything important. Just get on with routine and with preplanned tasks. (Of course, if you actually want a project to fail, a Void-of-Course Moon would be a good time to start it, from your point of view...!) You could also use the time for reflection, meditation and a review of what has been achieved over the past few days.

So make use of the following tables. They give the date and the time (in GMT only, so remember to add an hour to them when BST is operating) of the Moon's last aspect in a sign, and the date and time that she enters a new sign. Use the information well!

VOID-OF-COURSE MOON TABLES 2023

All times are GMT - add 1 hour for BST

From		To		From		To	
03 Jan	22.16	03 Jan	02.44	19 Mar	15.05	19 Mar	16.52
05 Jan	00.08	05 Jan	14.15	21 Mar	15.58	21 Mar	16.01
07 Jan	22.23	08 Jan	02.40	23 Mar	18.42	23 Mar	18.42
10 Jan	01.52	10 Jan	15.15	25 Mar	16.19	26 Mar	00.41
12 Jan	23.06	13 Jan	02.56	28 Mar	01.39	28 Mar	10.22
15 Jan	08.40	15 Jan	12.08	30 Mar	13.45	30 Mar	22.31
17 Jan	14.27	17 Jan	17.33				
19 Jan	10.09	19 Jan	19.11	02 Apr	06.03	02 Apr	10.57
21 Jan	15.52	21 Jan	18.29	04 Apr	13.50	04 Apr	21.51
23 Jan	10.19	23 Jan	17.36	06 Apr	12.43	07 Apr	06.29
25 Jan	16.11	25 Jan	18.48	09 Apr	09.09	09 Apr	12.57
27 Jan	21.01	27 Jan	23.42	11 Apr	10.48	11 Apr	17.33
30 Jan	05.52	30 Jan	08.35	13 Apr	14.14	13 Apr	20.42
				15 Apr	15.16	15 Apr	22.57
01 Feb	11.58	01 Feb	20.11	17 Apr	18.57	18 Apr	20.09
04 Feb	06.19	04 Feb	08.48	20 Apr	04.12	20 Apr	04.30
06 Feb	14.15	06 Feb	21.14	22 Apr	03.41	22 Apr	10.11
09 Feb	06.40	09 Feb	08.47	24 Apr	12.15	24 Apr	18.58
11Feb	16.41	11 Feb	18.34	26 Apr	23.41	27 Apr	06.30
13 feb	23.52	14 Feb	01.31	29 Apr	10.53	29 Apr	18.59
16 Feb	01.06	16 Feb	05.00				
18 Feb	04.18	18 Feb	05.35	01 May	23.53	02 May	06.09
20 Feb	02.00	20 Feb	04.56	04 May	09.17	04 May	14.32
22 Feb	04.05	22 Feb	05.14	06 May	14.38	06 May	20.04
24 Feb	07.22	24 Feb	08.29	08 May	20.28	08 May	23.33
26 Feb	14.42	26 Feb	15.48	10 May	23.52	11 May	02.05
				13 May	03.15	13 May	04.39
01 Mar	01.07	01 Mar	02.40	15 May	02.56	15 May	07.56
03 Mar	14.22	03 Mar	15.16	17 May	09.10	17 May	12.28
06 Mar	03.18	06 Mar	03.38	19 May	17.51	19 May	18.48
08 Mar	14.07	08 Mar	14.44	21 May	22.12	22 May	03.28
10 Mar	23.36	11 Mar	00.06	24 May	09.12	24 May	14.35
13 Mar	06.38	13 Mar	07.21	26 May	06.38	27 May	03.35
15 Mar	08.50	15 Mar	12.06	29 May	04.46	29 May	14.51
17 Mar	14.14	17 Mar	14.25	31 May	14.53	31 May	23.45

From		To	
From		*To*	
03 Jun	00.51	03 Jun	05.03
05 Jun	03.24	05 Jun	07.31
07 Jun	04.40	07 Jun	08.42
09 Jun	04.24	09 Jun	10.14
11 Jun	13.20	11 Jun	13.20
13 Jun	18.27	13 Jun	18.31
16 Jun	01.36	16 Jun	01.46
18 Jun	06.24	18 Jun	10.58
20 Jun	21.43	20 Jun	22.04
22 Jun	17.01	23 Jun	10.35
25 Jun	22.24	25 Jun	22.57
28 Jun	08.19	28 Jun	08.55
30 Jun	14.20	30 Jun	14.59
02 Jul	14.33	02 Jul	17.20
04 Jul	16.45	04 Jul	17.30
06 Jul	13.42	06 Jul	17.32
08 Jul	18.22	08 Jul	19.19
10 Jul	23.11	10 Jul	23.55
13 Jul	06.11	13 Jul	07.26
15 Jul	12.35	15 Jul	17.13
18 Jul	03.06	18 Jul	04.39
20 Jul	14.08	20 Jul	17.13
23 Jul	04.06	23 Jul	05.24
25 Jul	15.05	25 Jul	16.55
27 Jul	22.36	28 Jul	00.24
29 Jul	23.51	30 Jul	03.44
01 Aug	02.13	01 Aug	03.58
02 Aug	21.15	03 Aug	03.05
05 Aug	01.21	05 Aug	03.19
07 Aug	04.13	07 Aug	06.24
09 Aug	10.39	09 Aug	13.05
11 Aug	17.27	11 Aug	22.52
14 Aug	04.57	14 Aug	10.36
16 Aug	09.38	16 Aug	23.14
19 Aug	08.51	19 Aug	11.53
21 Aug	02316	21 Aug	23.22

From		To	
From		*To*	
24 Aug	05.10	24 Aug	08.07
26 Aug	11.56	26 Aug	13.05
28 Aug	11.49	28 Aug	14.32
30 Aug	03.04	30 Aug	13.56
01 Sep	10.36	01 Sep	12.25
03 Sep	11.57	03 Sep	15.00
05 Sep	16.46	05 Sep	20.07
07 Sep	22.22	08 Sep	05.00
10 Sep	12.47	10 Sep	16.36
12 Sep	15.06	13 Sep	05.18
15 Sep	13.49	15 Sep	17.44
18 Sep	01.06	18 Sep	04.58
20 Sep	10.21	20 Sep	14.06
22 Sep	19.32	22 Sep	20.20
24 Sep	20.45	24 Sep	23.29
26 Sep	12.39	27 Sep	00.18
28 Sep	20.58	29 Sep	00.17
30 Sep	21.49	01 Oct	01.18
03 Oct	01.20	03 Oct	05.03
05 Oct	06.34	05 Oct	12.32
07 Oct	19.12	07 Oct	23.24
10 Oct	09.37	10 Oct	12.02
12 Oct	20.10	13 Oct	00.22
15 Oct	07.01	15 Oct	11.04
17 Oct	15.44	17 Oct	19.38
19 Oct	19.02	20 Oct	01.55
22 Oct	06.00	22 Oct	06.06
23 Oct	19.04	24 Oct	08.33
26 Oct	06.39	26 Oct	10.02
28 Oct	08.20	28 Oct	11.44
30 Oct	11.36	30 Oct	15.08
01 Nov	12.36	01 Nov	21.30
04 Nov	03.28	04 Nov	07.21
06 Nov	07.25	06 Nov	19.39
09 Nov	04.55	09 Nov	08.08

From	To	From	To
11 Nov 15.05	11 Nov 18.39	06 Dec 13.50	06 Dec 16.35
13 Nov 23.03	14 Nov 02.23	09 Dec 01.05	09 Dec 03.35
15 Nov 22.57	16 Nov 04.33	11 Dec 08.57	11 Dec 11.11
18 Nov 08.27	11 Nov 11.27	13 Dec 06.48	13 Dec 15.31
20 Nov 10.50	20 Nov 14.29	15 Dec 16.04	15 Dec 17.56
22 Nov 15.10	22 Nov 17.19	17 Dec 12.04	17 Dec 19.58
24 Nov 17.40	24 Nov 20.29	19 Dec 21.03	19 Dec 22.47
26 Nov 21.52	27 Nov 00.40	22 Dec 02.47	22 Dec 02.50
29 Nov 01.03	29 Nov 06.54	24 Dec 06.40	25 Dec 08.15
		26 Dec 07.55	26 Dec 15.15
01 Dec 13.07	02 Dec 04.41	28 Dec 22.57	29 Dec 00.23
04 Dec 02.11	04 Dec 03.50	31 Dec 05.18	31 Dec 11.53

SUN & MOON RISE & SET TIMES 2023

These tables are accurate for the London area and for SE England generally; for other parts of the British Isles there will be several minutes' difference. There's no easy way to calculate the difference so if you want to find the exact times for your locality, go to the website
www.timeanddate.com/astronomy/

Note: ' --:-- ' in the Moon listings means that rising or setting occurs the next day.

Sun	Rise	Set	**Moon**	Rise	Set
01 Jan	08:06	16:02	01 Jan	12:35	02:50
02 Jan	08:06	16:03	02 Jan	12:50	04:09
03 Jan	08:05	16:04	03 Jan	13:10	05:27
04 Jan	08:05	16:06	04 Jan	13:37	06:42
05 Jan	08:05	16:07	05 Jan	14:15	07:49
06 Jan	08:05	16:08	06 Jan	15:06	08:45
07 Jan	08:04	16:09	07 Jan	16:09	09:26
08 Jan	08:04	16:11	08 Jan	17:20	09:56
09 Jan	08:03	16:12	09 Jan	18:35	10:17
10 Jan	08:03	16:13	10 Jan	19:49	10:33
11 Jan	08:02	16:15	11 Jan	21:03	10:45
12 Jan	08:01	16:16	12 Jan	22:16	10:55
13 Jan	08:01	16:18	13 Jan	23:31	11:04

All times given are GMT

Sun	Rise	Set	Moon	Rise	Set
14 Jan	08:00	16:19	14 Jan	--:--	11:13
15 Jan	07:59	16:21	15 Jan	00:48	11:24
16 Jan	07:58	16:22	16 Jan	02:09	11:37
17 Jan	07:57	16:24	17 Jan	03:35	11:55
18 Jan	07:56	16:26	18 Jan	05:05	12:21
19 Jan	07:55	16:27	19 Jan	06:32	13:02
20 Jan	07:54	16:29	20 Jan	07:47	14:06
21 Jan	07:53	16:31	21 Jan	08:41	15:31
22 Jan	07:52	16:32	22 Jan	09:16	17:08
23 Jan	07:51	16:34	23 Jan	09:39	18:47
24 Jan	07:49	16:36	24 Jan	09:56	20:20
25 Jan	07:48	16:38	25 Jan	10:08	21:49
26 Jan	07:47	16:39	26 Jan	10:19	23:13
27 Jan	07:45	16:41	27 Jan	10:30	--:--
28 Jan	07:44	16:43	28 Jan	10:42	00:36
29 Jan	07:43	16:45	29 Jan	10:56	01:57
30 Jan	07:41	16:46	30 Jan	11:14	03:16
31 Jan	07:40	16:48	31 Jan	11:38	04:33
01 Feb	07:38	16:50	01 Feb	12:13	05:43
02 Feb	07:37	16:52	02 Feb	13:00	06:42
03 Feb	07:35	16:54	03 Feb	14:00	07:27
04 Feb	07:33	16:55	04 Feb	15:09	08:00
05 Feb	07:32	16:57	05 Feb	16:23	08:23
06 Feb	07:30	16:59	06 Feb	17:38	08:40
07 Feb	07:28	17:01	07 Feb	18:52	08:53
08 Feb	07:27	17:03	08 Feb	20:06	09:03
09 Feb	07:25	17:05	09 Feb	21:20	09:12
10 Feb	07:23	17:06	10 Feb	22:35	09:21
11 Feb	07:21	17:08	11 Feb	23:54	09:31
12 Feb	07:19	17:10	12 Feb	--:--	09:42
13 Feb	07:18	17:12	13 Feb	01:16	09:57
14 Feb	07:16	17:14	14 Feb	02:42	10:19
15 Feb	07:14	17:16	15 Feb	04:08	10:51
16 Feb	07:12	17:17	16 Feb	05:27	11:42
17 Feb	07:10	17:19	17 Feb	06:29	12:55
18 Feb	07:08	17:21	18 Feb	07:11	14:26

All times are GMT

Sun	Rise	Set	Moon	Rise	Set
19 Feb	07:06	17:23	19 Feb	07:39	16:05
20 Feb	07:04	17:25	20 Feb	07:58	17:42
21 Feb	07:02	17:27	21 Feb	08:13	19:16
22 Feb	07:00	17:28	22 Feb	08:24	20:45
23 Feb	06:58	17:30	23 Feb	08:35	22:11
24 Feb	06:56	17:32	24 Feb	08:47	23:36
25 Feb	06:54	17:34	25 Feb	09:00	--:--
26 Feb	06:51	17:35	26 Feb	09:16	00:59
27 Feb	06:49	17:37	27 Feb	09:38	02:20
28 Feb	06:47	17:39	28 Feb	10:10	03:34
01 Mar	06:45	17:41	01 Mar	10:53	04:38
02 Mar	06:43	17:43	02 Mar	11:49	05:28
03 Mar	06:41	17:44	03 Mar	12:56	06:04
04 Mar	06:39	17:46	04 Mar	14:09	06:29
05 Mar	06:36	17:48	05 Mar	15:25	06:47
06 Mar	06:34	17:50	06 Mar	16:40	07:01
07 Mar	06:32	17:51	07 Mar	17:55	07:12
08 Mar	06:30	17:53	08 Mar	19:09	07:21
09 Mar	06:27	17:55	09 Mar	20:25	07:30
10 Mar	06:25	17:56	10 Mar	21:43	07:39
11 Mar	06:23	17:58	11 Mar	23:04	07:50
12 Mar	06:21	18:00	12 Mar	--:--	08:03
13 Mar	06:19	18:02	13 Mar	00:29	08:22
14 Mar	06:16	18:03	14 Mar	01:54	08:49
15 Mar	06:14	18:05	15 Mar	03:15	09:31
16 Mar	06:12	18:07	16 Mar	04:21	10:33
17 Mar	06:09	18:08	17 Mar	05:09	11:56
18 Mar	06:07	18:10	18 Mar	05:41	13:29
19 Mar	06:05	18:12	19 Mar	06:02	15:05
20 Mar	06:03	18:14	20 Mar	06:18	16:39
21 Mar	06:00	18:15	21 Mar	06:30	18:11
22 Mar	05:58	18:17	22 Mar	06:41	19:39
23 Mar	05:56	18:19	23 Mar	06:52	21:06
24 Mar	05:53	18:20	24 Mar	07:04	22:33
25 Mar	05:51	18:22	25 Mar	07:19	23:57
26 Mar	05:49	18:24	26 Mar	07:38	--:--

All times are GMT

Sun	Rise	Set	Moon	Rise	Set
27 Mar	05:47	18:25	27 Mar	08:06	01:17
28 Mar	05:44	18:27	28 Mar	08:44	02:28
29 Mar	05:42	18:29	29 Mar	09:36	03:24
30 Mar	05:40	18:30	30 Mar	10:41	04:05
31 Mar	05:38	18:32	31 Mar	11:53	04:34
01 Apr	05:35	18:34	01 Apr	13:08	04:55
02 Apr	05:33	18:35	02 Apr	14:23	05:09
03 Apr	05:31	18:37	03 Apr	15:39	05:21
04 Apr	05:29	18:39	04 Apr	16:54	05:30
05 Apr	05:26	18:40	05 Apr	18:10	05:39
06 Apr	05:24	18:42	06 Apr	19:28	05:48
07 Apr	05:22	18:44	07 Apr	20:50	05:58
08 Apr	05:20	18:45	08 Apr	22:15	06:10
09 Apr	05:17	18:47	09 Apr	23:42	06:27
10 Apr	05:15	18:49	10 Apr	--:--	06:51
11 Apr	05:13	18:51	11 Apr	01:05	07:28
12 Apr	05:11	18:52	12 Apr	02:17	08:23
13 Apr	05:09	18:54	13 Apr	03:09	09:39
14 Apr	05:06	18:56	14 Apr	03:45	11:07
15 Apr	05:04	18:57	15 Apr	04:08	12:40
16 Apr	05:02	18:59	16 Apr	04:25	14:13
17 Apr	05:00	19:01	17 Apr	04:37	15:42
18 Apr	04:58	19:02	18 Apr	04:48	17:10
19 Apr	04:56	19:04	19 Apr	04:58	18:37
20 Apr	04:54	19:06	20 Apr	05:10	20:03
21 Apr	04:52	19:07	21 Apr	05:23	21:30
22 Apr	04:50	19:09	22 Apr	05:40	22:53
23 Apr	04:48	19:11	23 Apr	06:04	--:--
24 Apr	04:45	19:12	24 Apr	06:37	00:10
25 Apr	04:43	19:14	25 Apr	07:24	01:14
26 Apr	04:41	19:16	26 Apr	08:25	02:03
27 Apr	04:40	19:17	27 Apr	09:35	02:37
28 Apr	04:38	19:19	28 Apr	10:49	03:00
29 Apr	04:36	19:20	29 Apr	12:05	03:16
30 Apr	04:34	19:22	30 Apr	13:20	03:29

All times are GMT

Sun	Rise	Set	Moon	Rise	Set
01 May	04:32	19:24	01 May	14:34	03:39
02 May	04:30	19:25	02 May	15:50	03:48
03 May	04:28	19:27	03 May	17:07	03:57
04 May	04:26	19:29	04 May	18:28	04:06
05 May	04:25	19:30	05 May	19:53	04:17
06 May	04:23	19:32	06 May	21:22	04:32
07 May	04:21	19:33	07 May	22:50	04:54
08 May	04:19	19:35	08 May	--:--	05:26
09 May	04:18	19:37	09 May	00:08	06:16
10 May	04:16	19:38	10 May	01:08	07:27
11 May	04:14	19:40	11 May	01:48	08:53
12 May	04:13	19:41	12 May	02:14	10:25
13 May	04:11	19:43	13 May	02:32	11:56
14 May	04:10	19:44	14 May	02:46	13:25
15 May	04:08	19:46	15 May	02:57	14:51
16 May	04:07	19:47	16 May	03:07	16:15
17 May	04:05	19:49	17 May	03:17	17:40
18 May	04:04	19:50	18 May	03:29	19:05
19 May	04:03	19:52	19 May	03:44	20:30
20 May	04:01	19:53	20 May	04:05	21:50
21 May	04:00	19:55	21 May	04:34	23:00
22 May	03:59	19:56	22 May	05:15	23:56
23 May	03:58	19:57	23 May	06:10	--:--
24 May	03:56	19:59	24 May	07:18	00:36
25 May	03:55	20:00	25 May	08:31	01:03
26 May	03:54	20:01	26 May	09:46	01:22
27 May	03:53	20:02	27 May	11:01	01:36
28 May	03:52	20:04	28 May	12:15	01:46
29 May	03:51	20:05	29 May	13:29	01:56
30 May	03:50	20:06	30 May	14:44	02:04
31 May	03:49	20:07	31 May	16:03	02:13
01 Jun	03:49	20:08	01 Jun	17:26	02:23
02 Jun	03:48	20:09	02 Jun	18:53	02:37
03 Jun	03:47	20:10	03 Jun	20:24	02:55
04 Jun	03:46	20:11	04 Jun	21:49	03:22
05 Jun	03:46	20:12	05 Jun	22:59	04:06

All times are GMT

Sun	Rise	Set	Moon	Rise	Set
06 Jun	03:45	20:13	06 Jun	23:47	05:10
07 Jun	03:45	20:14	07 Jun	--:--	06:35
08 Jun	03:44	20:15	08 Jun	00:18	08:08
09 Jun	03:44	20:16	09 Jun	00:39	09:42
10 Jun	03:44	20:16	10 Jun	00:54	11:12
11 Jun	03:43	20:17	11 Jun	01:05	12:38
12 Jun	03:43	20:18	12 Jun	01:15	14:02
13 Jun	03:43	20:18	13 Jun	01:26	15:25
14 Jun	03:43	20:19	14 Jun	01:37	16:49
15 Jun	03:42	20:19	15 Jun	01:50	18:12
16 Jun	03:42	20:20	16 Jun	02:09	19:33
17 Jun	03:42	20:20	17 Jun	02:34	20:47
18 Jun	03:42	20:20	18 Jun	03:10	21:48
19 Jun	03:43	20:21	19 Jun	04:00	22:33
20 Jun	03:43	20:21	20 Jun	05:04	23:05
21 Jun	03:43	20:21	21 Jun	06:16	23:26
22 Jun	03:43	20:21	22 Jun	07:31	23:42
23 Jun	03:43	20:21	23 Jun	08:46	23:53
24 Jun	03:44	20:22	24 Jun	09:59	--:--
25 Jun	03:44	20:22	25 Jun	11:12	00:03
26 Jun	03:45	20:21	26 Jun	12:25	00:12
27 Jun	03:45	20:21	27 Jun	13:40	00:20
28 Jun	03:46	20:21	28 Jun	14:59	00:30
29 Jun	03:46	20:21	29 Jun	16:23	00:41
30 Jun	03:47	20:21	30 Jun	17:52	00:56
01 Jul	03:47	20:20	01 Jul	19:20	01:19
02 Jul	03:48	20:20	02 Jul	20:39	01:54
03 Jul	03:49	20:20	03 Jul	21:38	02:49
04 Jul	03:50	20:19	04 Jul	22:17	04:07
05 Jul	03:50	20:19	05 Jul	22:43	05:41
06 Jul	03:51	20:18	06 Jul	23:00	07:18
07 Jul	03:52	20:18	07 Jul	23:13	08:53
08 Jul	03:53	20:17	08 Jul	23:23	10:23
09 Jul	03:54	20:16	09 Jul	23:34	11:50
10 Jul	03:55	20:15	10 Jul	23:45	13:14
11 Jul	03:56	20:15	11 Jul	23:57	14:37

All times are GMT

Sun	Rise	Set	Moon	Rise	Set
12 Jul	03:57	20:14	12 Jul	--:--	16:00
13 Jul	03:58	20:13	13 Jul	00:14	17:22
14 Jul	04:00	20:12	14 Jul	00:36	18:37
15 Jul	04:01	20:11	15 Jul	01:09	19:42
16 Jul	04:02	20:10	16 Jul	01:54	20:32
17 Jul	04:03	20:09	17 Jul	02:53	21:07
18 Jul	04:04	20:08	18 Jul	04:03	21:31
19 Jul	04:06	20:06	19 Jul	05:17	21:48
20 Jul	04:07	20:05	20 Jul	06:33	22:01
21 Jul	04:08	20:04	21 Jul	07:47	22:11
22 Jul	04:10	20:03	22 Jul	08:59	22:20
23 Jul	04:11	20:01	23 Jul	10:11	22:28
24 Jul	04:12	20:00	24 Jul	11:25	22:36
25 Jul	04:14	19:59	25 Jul	12:40	22:46
26 Jul	04:15	19:57	26 Jul	14:00	22:59
27 Jul	04:17	19:56	27 Jul	15:24	23:17
28 Jul	04:18	19:54	28 Jul	16:52	23:45
29 Jul	04:20	19:53	29 Jul	18:15	--:--
30 Jul	04:21	19:51	30 Jul	19:23	00:29
31 Jul	04:23	19:50	31 Jul	20:11	01:35
01 Aug	04:24	19:48	01 Aug	20:43	03:04
02 Aug	04:26	19:46	02 Aug	21:03	04:42
03 Aug	04:27	19:45	03 Aug	21:18	06:22
04 Aug	04:29	19:43	04 Aug	21:30	07:57
05 Aug	04:30	19:41	05 Aug	21:41	09:28
06 Aug	04:32	19:39	06 Aug	21:51	10:56
07 Aug	04:33	19:38	07 Aug	22:04	12:23
08 Aug	04:35	19:36	08 Aug	22:19	13:48
09 Aug	04:36	19:34	09 Aug	22:39	15:11
10 Aug	04:38	19:32	10 Aug	23:08	16:29
11 Aug	04:40	19:30	11 Aug	23:50	17:38
12 Aug	04:41	19:28	12 Aug	--:--	18:31
13 Aug	04:43	19:26	13 Aug	00:45	19:10
14 Aug	04:44	19:24	14 Aug	01:52	19:37
15 Aug	04:46	19:22	15 Aug	03:06	19:56
16 Aug	04:47	19:20	16 Aug	04:21	20:09

All times are GMT

Sun	Rise	Set	Moon	Rise	Set
17 Aug	04:49	19:18	17 Aug	05:36	20:20
18 Aug	04:51	19:16	18 Aug	06:49	20:28
19 Aug	04:52	19:14	19 Aug	08:01	20:36
20 Aug	04:54	19:12	20 Aug	09:14	20:45
21 Aug	04:55	19:10	21 Aug	10:28	20:54
22 Aug	04:57	19:08	22 Aug	11:45	21:05
23 Aug	04:59	19:06	23 Aug	13:06	21:20
24 Aug	05:00	19:04	24 Aug	14:30	21:42
25 Aug	05:02	19:02	25 Aug	15:53	22:17
26 Aug	05:03	18:59	26 Aug	17:07	23:11
27 Aug	05:05	18:57	27 Aug	18:03	--:--
28 Aug	05:07	18:55	28 Aug	18:41	00:28
29 Aug	05:08	18:53	29 Aug	19:05	02:02
30 Aug	05:10	18:51	30 Aug	19:22	03:41
31 Aug	05:11	18:48	31 Aug	19:35	05:20
01 Sep	05:13	18:46	01 Sep	19:47	06:55
02 Sep	05:15	18:44	02 Sep	19:57	08:28
03 Sep	05:16	18:42	03 Sep	20:09	09:58
04 Sep	05:18	18:39	04 Sep	20:23	11:27
05 Sep	05:19	18:37	05 Sep	20:42	12:54
06 Sep	05:21	18:35	06 Sep	21:08	14:17
07 Sep	05:23	18:33	07 Sep	21:45	15:31
08 Sep	05:24	18:30	08 Sep	22:36	16:30
09 Sep	05:26	18:28	09 Sep	23:41	17:13
10 Sep	05:27	18:26	10 Sep	--:--	17:43
11 Sep	05:29	18:24	11 Sep	00:53	18:03
12 Sep	05:30	18:21	12 Sep	02:09	18:18
13 Sep	05:32	18:19	13 Sep	03:24	18:29
14 Sep	05:34	18:17	14 Sep	04:38	18:38
15 Sep	05:35	18:14	15 Sep	05:51	18:46
16 Sep	05:37	18:12	16 Sep	07:04	18:54
17 Sep	05:38	18:10	17 Sep	08:18	19:03
18 Sep	05:40	18:07	18 Sep	09:34	19:13
19 Sep	05:42	18:05	19 Sep	10:54	19:26
20 Sep	05:43	18:03	20 Sep	12:17	19:45
21 Sep	05:45	18:00	21 Sep	13:39	20:14

All times are GMT

Sun	Rise	Set	Moon	Rise	Set
22 Sep	05:46	17:58	22 Sep	14:56	20:59
23 Sep	05:48	17:56	23 Sep	15:57	22:05
24 Sep	05:50	17:54	24 Sep	16:39	23:30
25 Sep	05:51	17:51	25 Sep	17:08	--:--
26 Sep	05:53	17:49	26 Sep	17:27	01:05
27 Sep	05:55	17:47	27 Sep	17:41	02:42
28 Sep	05:56	17:44	28 Sep	17:53	04:18
29 Sep	05:58	17:42	29 Sep	18:03	05:51
30 Sep	05:59	17:40	30 Sep	18:14	07:23
01 Oct	06:01	17:38	01 Oct	18:27	08:55
02 Oct	06:03	17:35	02 Oct	18:43	10:26
03 Oct	06:04	17:33	03 Oct	19:06	11:54
04 Oct	06:06	17:31	04 Oct	19:39	13:15
05 Oct	06:08	17:29	05 Oct	20:26	14:23
06 Oct	06:09	17:26	06 Oct	21:27	15:13
07 Oct	06:11	17:24	07 Oct	22:38	15:47
08 Oct	06:13	17:22	08 Oct	23:54	16:10
09 Oct	06:14	17:20	09 Oct	--:--	16:26
10 Oct	06:16	17:17	10 Oct	01:09	16:38
11 Oct	06:18	17:15	11 Oct	02:24	16:48
12 Oct	06:19	17:13	12 Oct	03:37	16:56
13 Oct	06:21	17:11	13 Oct	04:51	17:04
14 Oct	06:23	17:09	14 Oct	06:05	17:12
15 Oct	06:24	17:07	15 Oct	07:21	17:22
16 Oct	06:26	17:04	16 Oct	08:41	17:34
17 Oct	06:28	17:02	17 Oct	10:04	17:51
18 Oct	06:30	17:00	18 Oct	11:28	18:16
19 Oct	06:31	16:58	19 Oct	12:47	18:55
20 Oct	06:33	16:56	20 Oct	13:53	19:53
21 Oct	06:35	16:54	21 Oct	14:40	21:11
22 Oct	06:36	16:52	22 Oct	15:12	22:41
23 Oct	06:38	16:50	23 Oct	15:33	--:--
24 Oct	06:40	16:48	24 Oct	15:48	00:15
25 Oct	06:42	16:46	25 Oct	16:00	01:48
26 Oct	06:43	16:44	26 Oct	16:10	03:19
27 Oct	06:45	16:42	27 Oct	16:20	04:49

All times are GMT

Sun	Rise	Set	Moon	Rise	Set
28 Oct	06:47	16:40	28 Oct	16:32	06:20
29 Oct	06:49	16:38	29 Oct	16:46	07:51
30 Oct	06:50	16:37	30 Oct	17:06	09:22
31 Oct	06:52	16:35	31 Oct	17:34	10:49
01 Nov	06:54	16:33	01 Nov	18:15	12:06
02 Nov	06:56	16:31	02 Nov	19:12	13:05
03 Nov	06:57	16:29	03 Nov	20:20	13:46
04 Nov	06:59	16:28	04 Nov	21:36	14:14
05 Nov	07:01	16:26	05 Nov	22:52	14:33
06 Nov	07:03	16:24	06 Nov	--:--	14:46
07 Nov	07:05	16:23	07 Nov	00:07	14:56
08 Nov	07:06	16:21	08 Nov	01:21	15:05
09 Nov	07:08	16:19	09 Nov	02:34	15:13
10 Nov	07:10	16:18	10 Nov	03:47	15:21
11 Nov	07:12	16:16	11 Nov	05:03	15:30
12 Nov	07:13	16:15	12 Nov	06:22	15:41
13 Nov	07:15	16:13	13 Nov	07:45	15:56
14 Nov	07:17	16:12	14 Nov	09:11	16:19
15 Nov	07:18	16:11	15 Nov	10:34	16:54
16 Nov	07:20	16:09	16 Nov	11:46	17:46
17 Nov	07:22	16:08	17 Nov	12:40	19:00
18 Nov	07:24	16:07	18 Nov	13:15	20:27
19 Nov	07:25	16:06	19 Nov	13:39	21:59
20 Nov	07:27	16:04	20 Nov	13:55	23:30
21 Nov	07:28	16:03	21 Nov	14:08	--:--
22 Nov	07:30	16:02	22 Nov	14:18	00:59
23 Nov	07:32	16:01	23 Nov	14:28	02:27
24 Nov	07:33	16:00	24 Nov	14:39	03:54
25 Nov	07:35	15:59	25 Nov	14:51	05:23
26 Nov	07:36	15:58	26 Nov	15:08	06:52
27 Nov	07:38	15:57	27 Nov	15:32	08:21
28 Nov	07:39	15:57	28 Nov	16:07	09:43
29 Nov	07:41	15:56	29 Nov	16:57	10:51
30 Nov	07:42	15:55	30 Nov	18:02	11:41
01 Dec	07:44	15:55	01 Dec	19:16	12:14

All times are GMT

Sun	Rise	Set	Moon	Rise	Set
02 Dec	07:45	15:54	02 Dec	20:33	12:37
03 Dec	07:46	15:53	03 Dec	21:49	12:52
04 Dec	07:48	15:53	04 Dec	23:03	13:04
05 Dec	07:49	15:52	05 Dec	--:--	13:13
06 Dec	07:50	15:52	06 Dec	00:16	13:21
07 Dec	07:51	15:52	07 Dec	01:28	13:29
08 Dec	07:53	15:52	08 Dec	02:42	13:37
09 Dec	07:54	15:51	09 Dec	03:59	13:47
10 Dec	07:55	15:51	10 Dec	05:20	14:01
11 Dec	07:56	15:51	11 Dec	06:45	14:20
12 Dec	07:57	15:51	12 Dec	08:11	14:49
13 Dec	07:58	15:51	13 Dec	09:30	15:36
14 Dec	07:59	15:51	14 Dec	10:33	16:44
15 Dec	07:59	15:51	15 Dec	11:16	18:09
16 Dec	08:00	15:51	16 Dec	11:43	19:43
17 Dec	08:01	15:52	17 Dec	12:02	21:16
18 Dec	08:02	15:52	18 Dec	12:15	22:47
19 Dec	08:02	15:52	19 Dec	12:26	--:--
20 Dec	08:03	15:53	20 Dec	12:36	00:14
21 Dec	08:03	15:53	21 Dec	12:46	01:40
22 Dec	08:04	15:54	22 Dec	12:58	03:06
23 Dec	08:04	15:54	23 Dec	13:13	04:33
24 Dec	08:05	15:55	24 Dec	13:33	06:00
25 Dec	08:05	15:56	25 Dec	14:03	07:23
26 Dec	08:05	15:56	26 Dec	14:46	08:36
27 Dec	08:06	15:57	27 Dec	15:45	09:33
28 Dec	08:06	15:58	28 Dec	16:57	10:12
29 Dec	08:06	15:59	29 Dec	18:14	10:39
30 Dec	08:06	16:00	30 Dec	19:31	10:57
31 Dec	08:06	16:01	31 Dec	20:46	11:10

"A man is not dead while his name is still spoken."

~ Terry Pratchett

All times are GMT

January 2023

*"The wages of sin is death but so is the salary
of virtue, and at least the evil get to go home early
on Fridays."*

~ Terry Pratchett (Witches Abroad)

Sunday 1st

♀♂♀ 05.25   ☽△☉ 13.42   ☽♂♅ 21.52

All times are GMT

January 2023

"Clothes make the man. Naked people have little or no influence in society."

~ Mark Twain

1st	Euro Day (EU)
	Public Domain Day
	Shogatsu/Gantan-sai (Shinto)
	Jump-up Day (Montserrat)

Joe Orton, British playwright, b 1933

January 2023

Monday 2nd

☿✱♆ 06.44 ☽□♄ 12.15 ☽△☿ 12.30 ☽✱♆ 12.53 ☽△♀ 22.15

Tuesday 3rd

Venus enters Aquarius 02.09
Moon enters Gemini 02.44

☽△♀ 02.48 ☽✱♃ 05.37 ☽☌♂ 19.47

Wednesday 4th

♀✱♃ 09.08 ☽△♄ 23.54

Thursday 5th

Moon enters Cancer 14.15

☽□♆ 00.08 ☉△♅ 16.43 ☽□♃ 17.50

Friday 6th

◯ Full Moon 23:08

☽✱♅ 20.30 ☽☍☉ 23.08

Saturday 7th

☽☍☿ 01.36 ☽△♆ 12.30 ☉☌☿ 12.57 ☽☍♀ 22.23

Sunday 8th

Moon enters Leo 02.40

☽△♃ 07.00 ☽☍♀ 16.52 ☽✱♂ 19.19 ☿△♅ 23.23

All times are GMT

January 2023

2nd	**Handsel Monday (Scotland)** **Bank Holiday**

3rd	**Bank Holiday (Scotland only)** **Setsebun (Shinto)**

Greta Thurnberg, environmental campaigner, b 2003

4th	

5th	**Twelfth Night**

First performance of Samuel Beckett's play *Waiting for Godot* (in Paris) 1953

6th	**Feast of the Nativity (Orthodox Christian)** **Womens' Christmas (Ireland)** **Epiphany (Christian)** **Þrettándinn (Iceland)**

Maria Montessori, pioneering educator, opened her first school 1907

7th	**Christmas Day (Rastafarian, Orthodox Christianity)** **Distaff Day**

8th	**Typing Day**

Alfred Russel Wallace, British naturalist, biologist and explorer, b 1823

January 2023

Monday 9th

☽□♅ 9.02   ♀△♂ 15.22
Moon enters Virgo 15.15

Tuesday 10th

☽☌♄ 01.52

Wednesday 11th

☽□♂ 07.36   ☽△☿ 14.58   ☽△♅ 21.17
Mars goes direct

Thursday 12th

☽△☉ 11.07   ☽☌♆ 13.21   ☽△♀ 23.06
Moon enters Libra 02.56

Friday 13th

☽△♃ 08.34   ☉✳︎♆ 14.11   ☽△♂ 18.46   ☽□♆ 21.55

Saturday 14th

☽△♀ 05.58
Moon enters Scorpio 12.08

Sunday 15th
◑ Last Quarter 02:10

☽△♄ 00.47   ♀□♅ 01.22   ☽□☉ 02.10   ☽□♀ 08.40

All times are GMT

January 2023

9th   **Plough Monday**

Simone de Beauvoir, philosopher, writer and feminist activist, b 1908

10th

Jim Croce, American folk/rock singer and songwriter, b 1943

11th

12th   **Yennayer (Berber New Year)**

The UK's first supermarket opened (in Manor Park, London) 1948

13th   **Maghi (Sikh)**

14th   **World Logic Day**
Makar Sankranti (Hindu)

15th   **Parinirvana Day (Buddhist)**
Makar Sankranti (Hindu)
World Religion Day

Ivor Cutler, Scottish poet, singer, songwriter, storyteller, illustrator, b 1923

January 2023

Monday 16th

☽✶☿ 03.47 ☽☌♅ 15.17 ☽□♀ 19.09

Tuesday 17th

Moon enters Sagittarius 17.33

☽△♆ 05.48 ☽□♄ 07.27 ☽✶☉ 12.36 ☽✶♀ 14.27 ☽△♃ 23.41

Wednesday 18th

Mercury goes direct

☽☌♂ 07.49 ☉☌♀ 14.44

Thursday 19th

Moon enters Capricorn 19.11

☽✶♀ 03.05 ☽□♆ 08.17 ☽✶♄ 10.09

Friday 20th

Sun enters Aquarius 08.29

☽□♃ 01.29 ☽☌♀ 08.30 ☽△♅ 18.55

Saturday 21st

● New Moon 20:53

Moon enters Aquarius 18.29

☽✶♆ 08.01 ☽☌♀ 15.52 ☽☌☉ 20.53

Sunday 22nd

☽✶♃ 01.09 ☽△♂ 08.02 ☽✶♅ 17.49 ♀☌♄ 22.13

All times are GMT

January 2023

16th

17th   **Blessings of the Animals (Hispanic Christian)**

Robert Fludd, astrologer, mathematician and Qabalist, b 1574

18th

Robert Anton Wilson, US author, mystic and futurist, b 1932

19th   **Timkat (Ethiopian Christian)**

Janis Joplin, US rock/blues singer, b 1943

20th

21st

Grigori Rasputin, Russian mystic, b 1869

22nd   **Chinese New Year (Year of the Rabbit)**

January 2023

Monday 23rd   Moon enters Pisces 17.36

☽☌♄ 09.24   ☽☌♀ 10.19

Tuesday 24th

☽□♂ 07.56   ☽✳☿ 09.58   ☽✳♅ 17.43

Wednesday 25th   Moon enters Aries 18.48

☉✳♃ 01.30   ☽☌♆ 07.42   ☽✳♀ 16.11

Thursday 26th

☽☌♃ 03.18   ☽✳☉ 04.59   ☽✳♂ 10.40   ☽□♆ 15.08

Friday 27th   Venus enters Pisces 02.33
Moon enters Taurus 23.42

☽✳♄ 15.13   ☽□♀ 21.09

Saturday 28th
◑ First Quarter 15:19

☽✳♀ 01.56   ☽□☉ 15.19

Sunday 29th

☽△♀ 01.44   ☽☌♅ 03.37   ☽□♆ 20.22

All times are GMT

January 2023

23rd
Bounty Day (Pitcairn Islands)

Mosaic, the first graphical web browser, was launched 1993

24th

25th
Tatiana Day (Russia)
Burns Night (Scotland)

Aloha Wanderwell became the first woman to drive around the world 1927

26th
International Customs Day

27th
Holocaust Remembrance Day

28th
Data Privacy Day

29th

January 2023

Monday 30th

☽□♄ 00.03 ☉△♂ 01.45 ☿△ ♅ 02.16 ☽△♀ 05.52 ☽□♀ 07.54 ☽⚹♃ 20.01

Tuesday 31st

☽☌♂ 04.27 ☽△☉ 06.24

*"I used to sell furniture for a living. The trouble
was, it was my own."*

~ Les Dawson

All times are GMT

January 2023

30th	**Mahayana New Year (Buddhism)**

Zsuzsanna Budapest, founder of Dianic Wicca, b 1940

31st	**Up Helly Aa (Shetland Islands)**

"We delight in the beauty of the butterfly, but rarely admit the changes it has gone through to achieve that beauty."

~ Maya Angelou

February 2023

*"Love recognizes no barriers. It jumps hurdles,
leaps fences, penetrates walls to arrive at its
destination full of hope."*

~ Maya Angelou

Wednesday 1st   Moon enters Cancer 20.11

☽□♆ 07.21   ☽△♄ 11.58

Thursday 2nd

☽□♃ 08.55   ☽△♀ 12.15

Friday 3rd

☽✶♅ 02.27   ☽☌♀ 12.09 ☽△♆ 20.02

Saturday 4th   Moon enters Leo 08.04

☉□♅ 02.50   ☽☌♀ 06.19   ☽△♃ 22.34

Sunday 5th
○ Full Moon 18:29

♀□♂ 03.29   ☽✶♂ 07.35   ☽□♅ 15.08   ☽☌☉ 18.29

All times are GMT

Febuary 2023

"The one-eyed mollusc on the sea-bottom, feathered and luminous, is my equal in what he and I know of star clusters not yet found by the best of star-gazers."

~ Carl Sandburg

| 1st | **Imbolc (Pagan)**
Candlemas (Christian) |

| 2nd | **World Wetlands Day** |

| 3rd | Eva Cassidy, American singer, b 1963
Setsubun (Shinto) |

| 4th | Henning Mankell, Swedish crime novelist, b 1948
International Day of Human Fraternity
World Cancer Day |

| 5th | Ida Lupino, actress, singer and producer, b 1918
Runeberg's Birthday (Finland)
Lantern Festival (Chinese)
Thaipusam (Hindu) |

The *Hägar the Horrible* comic strip was first published, 1973

February 2023

Monday 6th	Moon enters Virgo 21.14

☽☌♄ 14.15   ♀⚹♆ 18.26

Tuesday 7th	

☽□♂ 21.05

Wednesday 8th	

☽☌♀ 03.01   ☽△♅ 03.36   ♀⚹♅ 05.29   ☽☌♆ 20.40

Thursday 9th	Moon enters Libra 08.47

☽△☿ 02.30   ☽△♀ 06.40

Friday 10th	

☽☌♃ 00.02   ☽△♂ 09.25   ☽☌♅ 17.16

Saturday 11th	Mercury enters Aquarius 11.22
	Moon enters Scorpio 18.34

☽△☉ 03.38   ☽△♄ 13.07   ☽□♀ 16.41   ☽□☿ 19.27

Sunday 12th	

☽☌♂ 04.21   ☽☌☿ 05.45   ☽△♆ 19.15

All times are GMT

February 2023

6th

St Brigid's Day (Ireland)
Sami National Day

7th

8th

Peter J. Carroll, occultist, author, founder of Chaos Magic theory, b 1953

9th

10th

11th

International Day of Women and Girls in Science
European 112 Day (EU)

12th

Red Hand Day
Darwin Day

Franco Zeffirelli, Italian film/opera/television director, b 1923

February 2023

Monday 13th
◑ Last Quarter 16:01

☽△♀ 10.16 ☽△♇ 14.49 ☽□☉ 16.01 ☽□♄ 2053 ☽✳♀ 23.52

Tuesday 14th
Moon enters Sagittarius 01.31

☽✳♀ 08.39 ☽△♃ 16.56

Wednesday 15th

☽☌♂ 02.06 ♀☌♇ 12.25 ☽□♇ 19.06 ☽□♀ 19.43

Thursday 16th
Moon enters Capricorn 05.00

☽✳☉ 00.03 ☽✳♄ 01.06 ☉☌♄ 16.48 ☽□♃ 20.11

Friday 17th

☽△♅ 05.55 ☽✳♇ 20.16

Saturday 18th
Moon enters Aquarius 05.35
Sun enters Pisces 22:34

☽✳♀ 01.06 ☿✳♃ 02.15 ☽☌♀ 04.18 ☽✳♃ 20.51 ☽☌♀ 22.35

Sunday 19th

☽□♅ 05.42 ☽△♂ 06.01 ♀✳♀ 17.05

All times are GMT

February 2023

13th   **World Radio Day**

14th

15th   **John Frum Day (Vanuatu)**
                                          Nirvana Day (Buddhist)
                                                  ENIAC Day

Susan B. Anthony, US suffragette leader, b 1820

16th

The first BBC radio drama was broadcast (a scene from *Julius Caesar*) 1923

17th

The Campaign for Nuclear Disarmament (CND) was founded in the UK 1958

18th   **Maha Shivaratri (Hindu)**
                                            Lilat al Miraj (Islam)

19th   **Wife's Day (Iceland)**

February 2023

Monday 20th

● New Moon 07:06

Moon enters Pisces 04.56
Venus enters Aries 07.56

☽☌♄ 02.00   ☽☌☉ 07.06

Tuesday 21st

☽✶♅ 05.20   ☽□♂ 06.44   ☽☌♆ 19.52   ☿□♅ 22.22

Wednesday 22nd

Moon enters Aries 05.14

☽✶♀ 04.05   ☽☍♀ 09.26   ☿△♂ 20.14   ☿☌♃ 22.48

Thursday 23rd

☽✶♂ 09.44   ☽✶☿ 11.03

Friday 24th

Moon enters Taurus 08.29

☽✶♄ 06.06   ☽□♅ 07.22   ☽✶☉ 19.02

Saturday 25th

☽☌♅ 12.24

Sunday 26th

Moon enters Gemini 15.48

☽☿ 00.16   ☽✶♆ 05.15   ☽□♄ 13.45   ☽△♅ 14.42

All times are GMT

February 2023

20th

World Social Justice day

21st

International Mother Language Day
Feralia (Roman)

The Communist Manifesto was published, in London, 1848

22nd

World Thinking Day (Girl Guides & Girl Scouts)
Start of Lent (Christian)

23rd

24th

25th

26th

February 2023

Monday 27th

◑ First Quarter 08:06

☽□☉ 08.06   ☽⚹♀ 08.24   ☽⚹♃ 14.08

Tuesday 28th

☽☌♂ 04.21   ☽□♆ 15.46   ☽△☿ 19.27

"If wealth was the inevitable result of hard work and enterprise, every woman in Africa would be a millionaire."

~ George Monbiot

All times are GMT

February 2023

27th

28th

*"I never forget a face - but in your case, I'll
be glad to make an exception."*

~ Groucho Marx

March 2023

"If only there were evil people somewhere insidiously committing evil deeds, and it were necessary only to separate them from the rest of us and destroy them. But the line dividing good and evil cuts through the heart of every human being. And who is willing to destroy a piece of his own heart?"

~ Aleksandr Solzhenitsyn, The Gulag Archipelago

Wednesday 1st　　　　　　　Moon enters Cancer 02.40

☽△♄ 01.07

Thursday 2nd　　　　　　Mercury enters Pisces 22.52

☽△☉ 01.10　☽□♀ 02.50　♀☌♃ 05.36　☽⚹♅ 10.03　♀☌♄ 13.34

Friday 3rd　　　　　　　Moon enters Leo 15.16

☽△♆ 04.23　☽☌♅ 14.22

Saturday 4th

☽△♃ 16.56　☽△♀ 22.28　☽□♅ 22.54

Sunday 5th

☽⚹♂ 09.26

All times are GMT

March 2023

Sometimes Haiku verse
makes no sense
at all to me.
Pass me that herring.

~ Anonymous

1st

Zero Discrimination Day
St Davids Day (Wales)
Beer Day (Iceland)

2nd

Arthur Machen, author and mystic, b 1863

3rd

World Hearing Day

4th

Patrick Moore, amateur astronomer, TV presenter and writer b 1923

5th

St. Pirans Day (Cornwall)

March 2023

Monday 6th	Moon enters Virgo 03.38

☽☌♄ 03.18   ☉✶♅ 13.42   ☽☌☿ 16.32

Tuesday 7th	Saturn enters Pisces 13:35
○ Full Moon 12:40	

☽△♅ 10.51   ☽☌☉ 12.40   ☽□♂ 23.06

Wednesday 8th	Moon enters Libra 14.44

☽☌♆ 04.39   ☽△♀ 14.07

Thursday 9th

☽☌♃ 17.27

Friday 10th

☽☌♀ 09.07   ☽△♂ 11.00   ☽□♀ 23.36

Saturday 11th	Moon enters Scorpio 00.06

☽△♄ 00.51   ♀✶♂ 15.05   ♀✶♅ 21.04

Sunday 12th

☽☌♅ 05.43   ☽△♀ 07.07   ☽△☉ 16.32   ☽△♆ 22.18

All times are GMT

March 2023

6th	European Day of the Righteous Day of the Dude (Dudism) Purim (Jewish)

Laurie Cabot, US Witchcraft High Priestess, b 1933

7th	

8th	International Women's Collaboration Brew Day International Womens Day Holi (Hindu)

9th	

Bobby Fischer, American-born Icelandic chess player, b 1943

10th	

11th	

12th	World Day Against Cyber Censorship Arbour Day (China) Aztec New Year

March 2023

Monday 13th

Moon enters Sagittarius 07.21

Tuesday 14th

☽✳♀ 06.58 ☽□♄ 08.34

Wednesday 15th
◑ Last Quarter 02:08

☽△♃ 09.57 ☽□☿ 21.58 ♂□♆ 23.39
Moon enters Capricorn 12.06

Thursday 16th

☽□☉ 02.08 ☽□♆ 03.38 ☽☌♂ 03.45 ☽△♀ 08.50 ☽✳♄ 13.41 ☉☌♆ 23.39
Venus enters Taurus 22.34

Friday 17th

☽□♃ 14.17 ☽△♅ 15.22 ☿☌♆ 17.13 ☉□♂ 18.10 ♀□☿ 19.59
Moon enters Aquarius 14.25

Saturday 18th

☿□♆ 04.48 ☽✳♆ 06.27 ☽✳☿ 08.28 ☽✳☉ 08.37
☉☌☿ 10.45 ☽☌♀ 14.44 ☽□☿ 15.50 ♀✳♄ 22.25

Sunday 19th

☽✳♃ 16.27 ☽□♅ 16.50
Mercury enters Aries 04.24
Moon enters Pisces 15.12

☿✳♀ 03.24 ☽△♂ 10.33 ☽☌♄ 17.28 ☽✳♀ 20.54

All times are GMT

March 2023

13th

14th   **Pi Day**

Diane Arbus, American photographer, b 1923

15th   **World Consumer Rights Day**

16th

Margot Adler, author and Wiccan priestess, b 1947

17th   **Bank Holiday (Northern Ireland only)**
                                                    St Patricks Day

---

18th   **Day of Equality (Finland)**

Comet Kohoutek was discovered by Czech astronomer Luboš Kohoutek 1973

19th   **Lailat al Bara'ah (Islam)**

March 2023

Monday 20th

Sun enters Aries 21:24

☽*♅ 17.33   ☉*♀ 20.12

Tuesday 21st

● New Moon 17:23

Moon enters Aries 16:01

☽☌♂ 08.20   ☽*♀ 15.58   ☽☌☉ 17.23

Wednesday 22nd

☽☌♀ 01.34   ☽☌♃ 20.17

Thursday 23rd

Pluto enters Aquarius 12.13
Moon enters Taurus 18.42

☽*♂ 17.13   ☽□♀ 18.42   ☽*♄ 21.57

Friday 24th

☽☌♀ 10N31   ☽☌♅ 23.52

Saturday 25th

Mars enters Cancer 11.45

☽*♆ 16.19

Sunday 26th

Moon enters Gemini 00.41

☽△♀ 00.46   ☽□♄ 04.38   ☽*☉ 11.03

All times are GMT

March 2023

20th	**SPRING EQUINOX** **Earth Day** **International Astrology Day** **Nowruz (Bahá'í, Zoroastrian)**

21st	**International Colour Day** **International Day of the Forest** **World Poetry Day**

Viv Stanshall, British singer, songwriter, musician, artist, poet, b 1943

22nd	**World Water Day**

Marcel Marceau, French mime artist and actor, b 1923

23rd	**Promised Messiah Day (Ahmadiyya)** **Start of Ramadan (Islam)**

24th	**World Tuberculosis Day**

Harry Houdini, escape artist, b 1874

25th	**Tolkien Reading Day** **Annunciation (Christian)**

26th	**Start of British Summer Time (clocks go forward)** **Khordad Sal (Zoroastrianism)**

BBC radio began broadcasting a daily weather forecast, 1923

March 2023

Monday 27th

$\mathcal{D} * \varphi$ 07.39 $\mathcal{D} * \mathcal{2}$ 19.57

Tuesday 28th

Moon enters Cancer 10.22

$\mathcal{D} \square \Psi$ 01.39 $\varphi \sigma \mathcal{2}$ 06.50 $\mathcal{D} \sigma \mathcal{O}'$ 13.19 $\mathcal{D} \triangle \hbar$ 15.03

Wednesday 29th
◑ First Quarter 02:32

$\mathcal{D} \square \odot$ 02.32 $\mathcal{D} * \varphi$ 16.15 $\mathcal{D} * \Ψ$ 19.40 $\mathcal{D} \square \mathcal{2}$ 23.35

Thursday 30th

Moon enters Leo 22.31

$\mathcal{D} \square \varphi$ 06.30 $\mathcal{D} \triangle \Psi$ 13.45 $\mathcal{O}' \triangle \hbar$ 19.03 $\varphi \sigma \Ψ$ 22N26 $\mathcal{D} \sigma^{\circ} \varphi$ 22.46

Friday 31st

$\mathcal{D} \triangle \odot$ 20.29

---

*"Only in our dreams are we free. The rest of the time
we need wages."*

~ Terry Pratchett (Wyrd Sisters)

All times are GMT

March 2023

27th   **World Theatre Day**

28th

29th

30th   **Maja Puja (Buddhism)**
Ram Navami (Hindu)

Albert Einstein's Unified Field Theory was published, 1953

31st   **World Backup Day**

"I used to believe in reincarnation - but that was in a previous life."

~ Steve Jones

April 2023

"The optimist proclaims that we live in the best of all possible worlds, and the pessimist fears this is true."

~ James Branch Cabell

Saturday 1st

☽□♅ 08.30   ☽□♀ 12.06   ☽△♃ 13.25

Sunday 2nd

Moon enters Virgo 10:57

☽△♀ 06.03   ☽☌♄ 1644   ☽✶♂ 1908

All times are GMT - add 1 hour to get BST times

April 2023

"Making money is good, but there are no pockets in a shroud."

~ Terry Pratchett (Raising Steam)

1st	**Kha b-Nisan (Assyrian New Year)** **Edible Book Day**

Sergei Rachmaninoff, Russian composer, pianist and conductor b 1973

2nd	**International Children's Book Day** **World Autism Awareness Day** **Fact-Checking Day**

April 2023

Monday 3rd
Mercury enters Taurus 16.22

☿□♇ 18.55 ☽△♅ 20.28

Tuesday 4th
Moon enters Libra 21.51

☽△♀ 06.04 ☽☍♆ 13.50 ☽△♇ 22.13

Wednesday 5th

☽□♂ 08.12 ☿✶♄ 16.21

Thursday 6th
◯ Full Moon 04.34

☽☍☉ 04.34 ☽☍♃ 12N43

Friday 7th
Moon enters Scorpio 06.29

☽□♇ 06.54 ☽ ♄ 12.44 ☽☍☿ 17.53 ♀✶♆ 17.58 ☽△♂ 18.42

Saturday 8th

♀✶♂ 06.29 ☽☍♅ 13.56

Sunday 9th
Moon enters Sagittarius 12.57

☽△♆ 05.50 ☽☍♀ 09.09 ☽✶♇ 13.33 ☽□♄ 19.21

All times are GMT - add 1 hour to get BST times

April 2023

3rd

4th

CND held its first Aldermaston Peace March 1958

5th
Qingming Festival (Chinese)
First day of Passover (Jewish)

6th

7th
Bank Holiday
Good Friday (Christian)
World Health Day

8th
International Romani Day

British horror writer James Herbert b 1943

9th
Easter Sunday (Christian)

Paul Robeson, US singer, actor and activist, b 1898

April 2023

Monday 10th

There are no major mundane aspects today

Tuesday 11th

Venus enters Gemini 04.47
Moon enters Capricorn at 17.33

☽△☉ 01.48   ☽△♃ 02.55   ♀△♀ 10.14   ☽□♆ 10.48   ☉♂♃ 22.07

Wednesday 12th

☽⚹♄ 00.08   ☽☌♂ 09.03   ☽ ☿ 13.35   ☽△♅ 23.24

Thursday 13th
◐ Last Quarter 09:11

Moon enters Aquarius 20.42

☽□♃ 07.20   ☽□☉ 09.11   ☽⚹♆ 14.14   ☽☌♀ 22.11

Friday 14th

☽△♀ 02.23   ♀□♄ 16.38   ☽□☿ 19.16

Saturday 15th

Moon enters Pisces 22.57

☽□♅ 02.08   ☽⚹♃ 10.36   ☽⚹☉ 15.16

Sunday 16th

☽☌♄ 05.58   ☽□♀ 08.58   ☽△♂ 17.49   ☽⚹☿ 23.24

All times are GMT - add 1 hour to get BST times

April 2023

10th **Feast of the Third Day of the Writing of the Book of the Law (Thelema)**
International Siblings Day
Bank Holiday (except Scotland)

Vodou recognised as a religion by Haiti 2003

11th **World Parkinson's Day**

Anton LaVey, founder of the Church of Satan, b 1930

12th **Yuri's Night**

Jeremy Beadle, UK TV presenter, b 1948

13th

The controversial covert Project MKUltra was launched by the CIA 1953

14th **Vaisakhi (Sikh)**

The Human Genome Project was completed 2003

15th **Universal day of Culture**
World Art Day

16th **Palm Sunday (Orthodox Christianity)**
Easter (Western Christianity)
World Voice Day

Margot Adler, US Wiccan priestess, broadcaster and writer, b 1946

April 2023

Monday 17th

Tuesday 18th

☽✶♅ 04.25 ☽☌♆ 18.57
Moon enters Aries 01.09

Wednesday 19th

☽✶♀ 01.41 ☽✶♀ 15.46 ☽✶♂ 22.16

Thursday 20th

● New Moon 04:12
Total Solar Eclipse

☽☌♃ 11.27
Moon enters Taurus 04.30
Sun enters Taurus 08:14

Friday 21st

☽☌☉ 04.12 ☽☐♀ 05.04 ☽✶♄ 12.30 ☉☐♀ 16.27
Mercury goes retrograde (until 15th May)

Saturday 22nd

☽✶♂ 04.36 ☽☌♀ 08.05 ☽☌♅ 12.09
Moon enters Gemini 10.11

Sunday 23rd

☽☐♆ 0341 ☽△♀ 10.49 ☽☐♄ 19.00

☽☌♀ 12.43

All times are GMT - add 1 hour to get BST times

April 2023

17th	**Hocktide Monday (Hungerford)** **World Hemophilia Day**

Lyndsay Anderson, UK film and theatre director, b 1923

18th	**Lailat al Qadr (Islam)**

19th	**Vesak (Buddhist)**

20th	**Sumardaggerin Fyrsti (Iceland)** **Chinese Language Day**

21st	**Holy Friday Orthodox Christian)** **First Day of Ridvan (Bahá'í)** **Grounation Day (Rastafari)**

22nd	**Eid -al-Fitr (Islam)** **Earth Day**

23rd	**International Pixel-Stained Technopeasant Day** **St Georges Day (England)** **World Book and Copyright Day**

April 2023

Monday 24th   Moon enters Cancer 18.58

☿∗♂ 03.19   ☽∗♃ 03.49   ☽□♆ 12.15

Tuesday 25th

☽∗☉ 04.11   ☽△♄ 04.40   ☉∗♄ 10.38   ☽∗☿ 23.47

Wednesday 26th

☽☌♂ 03.08   ☽∗♅ 06.45   ☽□♃ 21.09   ☽△♆ 23.41

Thursday 27th   Moon enters Leo 06.30
◑ First Quarter 21:20

☽☌♀ 07.13   ☽□☉ 21.20

Friday 28th

☽□☿ 09.44   ☽□♅ 19.26   ☽∗♀ 23.42

Saturday 29th   Moon enters Virgo 18.59

☽△♃ 10.53   ♂∗♅ 20.05

Sunday   30th

☽☌♄ 05.41   ☽△☉ 14.59   ☽△☿ 19.05

All times are GMT - add 1 hour to get BST times

April 2023

24th

25th

World Penguin Day

Walter de la Mare, British novelist, b 1873

26th

World Intellectual Property Day

27th

Mary Wollstonecraft, writer and advocate of women's rights, b 1759

28th

Sir Terry Pratchett b 1948

29th

Ninth Day of Ridvan (Bahá'í)
International Dance Day

30th

International Jazz Day
Walpurgis Night
Beltane Eve

The Bristol Bus Boycott, protesting racial discrimination, began 1963

May 2023

Monday 1st

Pluto goes retrograde until 11th October

☽△♅ 07.38   ☽⚹♂ 09.08   ☉☌☿ 23.28   ☽☍♆ 23.58

Tuesday 2nd

Moon enters Libra 06.09

☽△♀ 06.41

Wednesday 3rd

☽□♂ 21.10

Thursday 4th

Moon enters Scorpio 14.32

☽△♀ 07.54   ☽☌♃ 09.17   ☽□♀ 15.12   ♀□♆ 17.40

Friday 5th
○ Full Moon 17:34
Penumbral Lunar Eclipse

☽□♄ 00.53   ♀⚹♃ 04.03   ☽☍☉ 17.34

Saturday 6th

Moon enters Sagittarius 20.04

☽☍♅ 00.13   ☽△♂ 05.51   ☽△♆ 14.38   ☽⚹♀ 20.41

Sunday 7th

Venus enters Cancer 14.25

☽□♄ 06.12

All times are GMT - add 1 hour to get BST times

May 2023

1st

International Guerilla Gardening Day
Bank Holiday
BELTANE

Joseph Heller, US novelist, b 1923

2nd

International Harry Potter Day
World Press Freedom Day
World Asthma Day

The firs modern sighting of the Loch Ness Monster was reported 1933

3rd

James Brown, US songwriter, singer and musician, b 1928

4th

World Naked Gardening Day
International Firefighters Day
Star Wars Day

Chris Packham, naturalist and wildlife presenter, b 1961

5th

International Midwives' Day
Cinco de Mayo (Mexico)

Blind Willie McTell, blues/ragtime singer and guitarist, b 1898

6th

Furry Dance (Helston, Cornwall)

7th

May 2023

Monday 8th

☽□♆ 18.22 ☽△♃ 20.28

Tuesday 9th

Moon enters Capricorn 23.33

☽☌♀ 02.20 ☽✶♄ 09.39 ☉☌♅ 19.56

Wednesday 10th

☽△♅ 07.32 ☽△☉ 08.20 ☽☌♂ 16.38 ☽✶♆ 21.03 ☽□♃ 23.52

Thursday 11th

Moon enters Aquarius 02.05

☽☌♀ 02.40 ☽□☿ 12.45

Friday 12th

◐ Last Quarter 14:28

☿✶♄ 08.42 ☽□♅ 10.12 ☽□☉ 14.28

Saturday 13th

Moon enters Pisces 04.39

☿✶♀ 02.44 ☽✶♃ 03.15 ♀△♄ 15.50 ☽✶☿ 14.43 ☽☌♄ 15.12 ☽△♀ 15.50

Sunday 14th

☽✶♅ 13.22 ☽✶☉ 21.17

All times are GMT - add 1 hour to get BST times

May 2023

8th

World Red Cross and Red Crescent Day
White Lotus Day (Theosophy)

9th

10th

11th

12th

International ME/CFS and Fibromyalgia Awareness Day

13th

Abbotsbury Garland Day (Dorset)
World Fair Trade Day

14th

Jack Bruce, Scottish singer, songwriter and guitarist, b 1943

May 2023

Monday 15th
Moon enters Aries 07.56

☽△♂ 02.30   ☽♂♆ 02.56   ☽⚹♀ 08.29   ♂△♆ 13.44   ☽□♀ 23.41

Tuesday 16th
Jupiter enters Taurus 17.20

There are no major mundane aspects today

Wednesday 17th
Moon enters Taurus 12.28

☽□♂ 09.10   ☽♂♃ 12.47   ☽□♀ 13.00   ☽♂♀ 23.57   ☽⚹♄ 23.57

Thursday 18th

♃□♀ 01.11   ☉⚹♆ 09.00   ☽⚹♀ 09.18   ☽♂♅ 23.28

Friday 19th
Moon enters Gemini 18.48

● New Moon 15:53

☿⚹♄ 06.40   ☽⚹♆ 13.39   ☽♂☉ 15.53   ☽⚹♂ 17.51   ☽△♀ 19.20

Saturday 20th
Mars enters Leo 15:31

☽□♄ 06.58

Sunday 21st
Sun enters Gemini 07:09

♂☍♀ 03.12   ☉△♀ 13.58   ☽□♆ 22.12

All times are GMT - add 1 hour to get BST times

May 2023

15th   **International Conscientious Objectors Day**
                                    International Day of Families

---

16th

17th   **World Information Society Day**

18th   **International Museum Day**

Helen Sharman became the first British woman in space 1991

19th

Victoria Wood, British comedian, b 1953

20th   **Levellers Day (Burford, Oxfordshire)**
                                       World Metrology Day
                                           World Bee Day

21st   **International Tea Day**

May 2023

Monday 22nd	Moon enters Cancer 03.28

☽✶♃ 05.54 ☉✶♂ 05.57 ☽△♄ 16.24 ☽✶☿ 19.07

Tuesday 23rd

♂□♃ 05.13 ☽☌♀ 12.45 ☽✶♅ 18.07

Wednesday 24th	Moon enters Leo 14.35

☽△♆ 09.12 ☽☍♀ 15.04 ☽✶☉ 21.31

Thursday 25th

☽□☿ 10.11

Friday 26th

☽□♅ 06.38 ♀✶♅ 07.37

Saturday 27th	Moon enters Virgo 03:05
◑ First Quarter 15.22	

☽△♃ ☽□☉ 15.22 ☽2♄ 16.53

Sunday 28th

☽△☿ 03.07 ☉✶♄ 10.46 ☽△♅ 19.12

All times are GMT - add 1 hour to get BST times

May 2023

22nd

International Day for Biological Diversity
World Goth Day

23rd

World Turtle Day

Elias Ashmole, alchemist, b 1617

24th

Declaration of the Bab (Baha'i)

25th

Shauvot (Jewish)
Africa Day
Wear The Lilac Day
Geek Pride Day
Towel Day

26th

27th

Cilla Black, pop singer and TV presenter, b 1943

28th

Menstrual Hygiene Day
Pentecost (Christianity)

May 2023

Monday 29th	Moon enters Libra 14.51

☽✶♀ 00.19   ☽☌♆ 09.46   ☽△♀ 15.13

Tuesday 30th	

☽✶♂ 01.21   ☽△☉ 07.39

Wednesday 31st	Moon enters Scorpio 23.45

☽□♀ 14.53

*"When people talk about travelling to the past, they
worry about radically changing the present by doing
something small, but barely anyone in the present
really thinks that they can radically change the future
by doing something small."*

~ Unknown

May 2023

29th	**Ascension of Baha'u'llah (Baha'i)**
	Castleton Garland Day (Derbyshire)
	Oak Apple Day
	Bank Holiday

30th

Helen Sharman, first British woman in space, b 1963

31st   **World No Tobacco Day**

John Bonham, British rock drummer, b 1948

---

*"When my wife is upset over something, I let her colour
in my black-and-white tattoos. So she always has a
shoulder to crayon."*

~ Anonymous

June 2023

*"It is a well-known fact that those people who most
want to rule people are, ipso facto, those least
suited to do it. Anyone who is capable of getting
themselves made President should on no account be
allowed to do the job."*

~ Douglas Adams

Thursday 1st

☽□♀ 00.02   ☽☌♃ 06.04   ☽✳♂ 12.11   ☽△♄ 12.30

Friday 2nd

☽☌♀ 06.53   ☽☌♅ 12.10   ♀△♉ 22.42

Saturday 3rd

Moon enters Sagittarius 05.03

☽△♉ 00.42   ☽△♀ 00.51   ☽✳♀ 05.16   ☽□♄ 17.07   ☽△♂ 18.59

Sunday 4th
○ Full Moon 03:42

☽☌☉ 03.42   ☿☌♅ 19.49

June 2023

*"The presence of those seeking the truth is
infinitely to be preferred to the presence of
those who think they've found it."*

~ Terry Pratchett

1st
World Milk Day
Childrens Day

2nd

Alessandro Cagliostro, occultist, b 1743
3rd
Festival of Bellona (Roman)
World Bicycle Day

4th

June 2023

Monday 5th

Moon enters Capricorn 07.31
Venus enters Leo 13.46

☽□♆ 03.24 ☽△♃ 14.44 ♀☍♇ 16.05 ☽✶♄ 19.12

Tuesday 6th

☽△♅ 17.10 ☽△☿ 21.34

Wednesday 7th

Moon enters Aquarius 08.42

☽✶♆ 04.40 ☽☌♇ 08.48 ☽☍♀ 11.39 ☽□♃ 16.34

Thursday 8th

☽☍♂ 02.11 ☽△☉13.29 ☽□♅ 18.37

Friday 9th

Moon enters Pisces 10:14

☽□☿ 04.24 ☽✶♃ 19.02 ☿✶♆ 21.14 ☽☌♄ 22.16

Saturday 10th

◑ Last Quarter 19:31

☽□☉ 19.31 ☽✶♅ 21.21

Sunday 11th

Pluto enters Capricorn 09.47
Mercury enters Gemini 10.27
Moon enters Aries 13.20

☽☌♆ 09.09☿△♇ 10.26 ☽✶♇ 13.20 ☽✶☿ 23.43 ♀□♃ 15.39 ☽△♀ 23.40

All times are GMT - add 1 hour to get BST times

June 2023

5th   **World Environment Day**

6th

Alex Sanders, founder of Alexandrian Wicca, b 1926

7th

Prince, American singer,/songwriter b 1958

8th   **World Brain Tumour Day**
                                               World Oceans Day

Marguerite Yourcenar, French writer and poet, b 1903

9th

Elizabeth Garrett Anderson, first British woman to qualify as a doctor, b 1836

10th   **World Art Nouveau Day**

NASA launched *Spirit,* the first Mars rover, 2003

11th

Gene Wilder, US comedian, actor, writer and director. b 1933

June 2023

Monday 12th

$\mathcal{D} \triangle \mathcal{O}^{\!\!\!\!\text{ }}$ 12.35

Tuesday 13th

Moon enters Taurus 18.31

$\mathcal{D} \ast \odot$ 03.59 $\mathcal{D} \square \mathcal{Q}$ 18.27

Wednesday 14th

$\mathcal{D} \sigma \mathcal{L}$ 05.40 $\mathcal{D} \ast \mathcal{h}$ 07.36 $\mathcal{D} \square \mathcal{Q}$ 09.08 $\mathcal{D} \square \mathcal{O}^{\!\!\!\!\text{ }}$ 21.15

Thursday 15th

$\mathcal{D} \sigma \mathcal{H}$ 08.55 $\mathcal{Q} \square \mathcal{h}$ 16.09 $\mathcal{D} \ast \Psi$ 21.19

Friday 16th

Moon enters Gemini 01.46

$\mathcal{D} \triangle \mathcal{Q}$ 01.36 $\mathcal{D} \square \mathcal{h}$ 15.20 $\mathcal{D} \sigma \mathcal{Q}$ 19.12 $\mathcal{D} \ast \mathcal{Q}$ 20.57

Saturday 17th

Saturn goes retrograde until 4th November

$\mathcal{D} \ast \mathcal{O}^{\!\!\!\!\text{ }}$ 08.14 $\mathcal{Q} \ast \mathcal{Q}$ 15.29

Sunday 18th

Moon enters Cancer 10.58

● New Moon 04:37

$\mathcal{D} \sigma \odot$ 04.37 $\mathcal{D} \square \Psi$ 06.24

All times are GMT - add 1 hour to get BST times

June 2023

12th

13th **International Albinism Awareness Day**

Pioneer 10 became the first space craft to leave the Solar System 1983

14th **World Blood Donor Day**

15th **Global Wind Day**
National Beer Day

Alice Bailey, Theosophist, b 1888

16th **Bloomsday (Dublin)**
Sussex Day

Soviet cosmonaut Valentina Tereshkova became the first woman in space 1963

17th

MC Escher, Dutch graphic artist, 1898

18th **International Surfing Day**
Autistic Pride Day

Sally Ride became the first American woman in space 1983

June 2023

Monday 19th

☽∗♃ 00.45 ☽△♄ 01.00 ☉□♆ 03.54 ♃∗♄ 15.53

Tuesday 20th

Moon enters Leo 22.04

☽∗♅ 04.33 ☽△♆ 17.24 ☽☍♀ 21.43

Wednesday 21st

Sun enters Cancer 14.58

☽□♃ 13.15 ☿∗♂ 15.23

Thursday 22nd

Venus enters Gemini 00:34

☽♂♀ 03.08 ☽♂♂ 21.41 ☽☿ 15.51 ☽□♅ 17.01

Friday 23rd

Moon enters Virgo 10.35

☽∗☉ 14.24

Saturday 24th

☽☍♄ 01.07 ☽△♃ 02.53

Sunday 25th

Moon enters Libra 22.57

☽△♅ 05.53 ☽☍♆ 18.20 ☽△♀ 22.24 ☿□♆ 22.36

All times are GMT - add 1 hour to get BST times

June 2023

19th
New Church Day (Swedenborgian Christian)
World Sickle Cell Day

Theatrical premier of *The Rocky Horror Show* 1973

20th
World Refugee Day

The Wikimedia Foundation (publishers of Wikipedia) was founded 2003

21st
SUMMER SOLSTICE
Litha (Pagan)
World Humanism Day
First Nations Day

22nd
Dragon Boat Festival (Chinese)
Windrush Day

23rd
International Widows Day
St Johns Eve

The online world *Second Life* was launched 2003

24th
Bannockburn Day (Scotland)
Fors Fortuna Festival (Roman)

Start of the Battle of Bamber Bridge (Lancashire) 1943

25th
World Vitiligo Day

George Michael, singer, b 1963

June 2023

Monday 26th
◐ First Quarter 07:50

☽□☉ 07.50   ♂⚹♅ 09.23

Tuesday 27th
Mercury enters Cancer 00.24

☽⚹♀ 10.56   ☽⚹♂ 18.26

Wednesday 28th
Moon enters Scorpio 08.55

☽□♀ 08.19   ☽△☿ 15.32   ☽△☉ 21.49   ☽△♄ 22.07

Thursday 29th

☽☌♃ 01.29   ☉△♄ 01.43   ☽□♀ 21.32

Friday 30th
Neptune goes retrograde until 6th December
Moon enters Sagittarius 14.59

☽☌♅ 00.22   ☽□♂ 04.05   ☿△♄ 06.24   ☽△♆ 10.58   ☽⚹♀ 14.20

"The law, in its majestic equality, forbids rich and poor alike to sleep under bridges, beg in the streets and steal loaves of bread."

~ Anatole France

June 2023

26th   **Ratcatcher's Day (Hamelin, Germany)**

27th

28th   **Waqf al Arafa (Islam)**

Stewart Farrar, writer and Alexandrian High Priest, b 1916
29th   **Eid-al-Adha (Islam)**

30th   **Asteroid Day**

"When you learn, teach. When you get, give."
~ Maya Angelou

July 2023

*"I'm sure wherever my Dad is, he's looking down on us.
He's not dead, just very condescending."*

~ Jack Whitehall

Saturday 1st

☽□♄ 03.08   ☉☌☿ 05.06   ☿✳♃ 07.10   ☉✳♃ 10.26

Sunday 2nd

Moon enters Capricorn 17.20

☽△♀ 03.21   ☽△♂ 09.19   ☽□♆ 12.33   ♀□♅ 14.33

All times are GMT - add 1 hour to get BST times

July 2023

"Without a doubt it is more comfortable to endure blind bondage than to work for one's liberation."

~ Simone de Beauvoir

1st

George Sand, French novelist, memoirist, and journalist, b 1804

2nd

July 2023

Monday 3rd
○ Full Moon 11:39

☽✶♄ 04.43　☽△♃ 09.02　☽☌☉ 11.39　☽☌☿ 16.50

Tuesday 4th
Moon enters Aquarius 17.30

☽△♅ 04.30　☽✶♆ 13.49　☽☌♀ 16.45

Wednesday 5th

☽□♃ 09.28

Thursday 6th
Moon enters Pisces 17.32

☽□♅ 04.30　☽☌♀ 07.37　☽☌♂ 13.42

Friday 7th

♂♄ 04N47　☿✶♅ 04.54　☽✶♃ 10.28　☽△☉ 18.48

Saturday 8th
Moon entersAries 19.19

☽✶♅ 05.48　☽△☿ 09.55　☽☌♆ 15.21 ☽✶♀ 18.22

Sunday 9th

☿△♆ 23.57

All times are GMT - add 1 hour to get BST times

July 2023

3rd

4th

5th

Tynwald Day (Isle of Man)

The Isle of Man issued its first postage stamps 1973

6th

7th

World Chocolate Day

NASA launched the Opportunity Mars rover 2003

8th

9th

July 2023

Monday 10th
◑ Last Quarter 01:48

Mars enters Virgo 11.40
Moon enters Taurus 23.55

☽□☉ 01.48   ☽△♀ 16.34   ☿☌♀ 20.48   ☽□♀ 22.50   ☽□☿ 23.11

Tuesday 11th

Mercury enters Leo 04.11

☽△♂ 00.31   ☽✶♄ 12.11   ☽☌♃ 20.04

Wednesday 12th

☽✶☉ 12.30   ☽☌♅ 16.42

Thursday 13th

Moon enters Gemini 07.26

☽□♀ 01.24   ☽✶♆ 02.59   ☽△♀ 06.11   ☽□♂ 10.51   ☽✶☿ 16.40   ☽□♄ 20.06

Friday 14th

☉✶♅ 23.02

Saturday 15th

Moon enters Cancer 17.13

☽✶♀ 12.27   ☽□♆ 12.35

Sunday 16th

☽△♄ 06.06   ☽✶♃ 16.23

All times are GMT - add 1 hour to get BST times

July 2023

10th

Martyrdom of the Bab (Baha'i)
Nikola Tesla Day

11th

William Blackstone, English judge, lawyer and politician b 1723

12th

Bank Holiday (Northern Ireland only)
World Population Day

13th

Obon (Buddhist/Shinto)

14th

John Dee. mathematician, astronomer, astrologer, alchemist, b 1527

15th

16th

Sir Joshua Reynolds, Potrait artist, b 1723

July 2023

Monday 17th

● New Moon 18:32

☿□♃ 12.49 ☽⚹♅ 13.21 ☽☌☉ 18.32 ☽△♆ 23.52

Tuesday 18th

Moon enters Leo 04.39

☽☌♀ 03.06

Wednesday 19th

☽□♃ 05.02 ☽☌♀ 11.23

Thursday 20th

Moon enters Virgo 17.13

☽□♅ 01.51 ☉△♆ 13.07 ☽☌♀ 14.08 ♂☍♄ 20.39

Friday 21st

☽☍♄ 06.03 ☽☌♂ 06.36 ☽△♃ 18.13

Saturday 22nd

☉☍♀ 03.53 ☽△♅ 14N48

Sunday 23rd

Venus goes retrograde until 15th September
Sun enters Leo 01.50
Moon enters Libra 05.54

☽☍♆ 01.00 ☽△♀ 04.06 ☽⚹☉ 06.14 ☿□♅ 21.39

All times are GMT - add 1 hour to get BST times

July 2023

17th

World Day for International Justice

John Cooper, British racing car designer, b 1923

18th

Nelson Mandela Day

The chemical element Polonium was discovered by Marie & Pierre Curie 1898

19th

Islamic New Year (Hijri 1445)

20th

International Chess day

21st

World's lowest temperature (-89.2°C) was recorded, in Antarctica, 1983

22nd

Pi Approximation Day
Ratcatchers Day

23rd

July 2023

Monday 24th

There are no major mundane aspects today

Tuesday 25th
◐ First Quarter 22:07

Moon enters Scorpio 16.55

☽✶☿ 06.39   ☽✶♀ 14.00   ☽□♀ 15.05   ☽□☉ 22.07

Wednesday 26th

☽△♄ 04.27   ☽✶♂ 11.31   ☽☌♃ 17.38

Thursday 27th

☽☌♅ 11.10   ☿☌♀ 15.16   ☽△♆ 19.56   ☽□♀ 21.06   ☽□☿ 21.53

Friday 28th

Moon enters Sagittarius 00.24
Mercury enters Virgo 21.31

☽△☉ 09.22   ☽□♄ 10.52   ☽□♂ 20.09

Saturday 29th

☽□♆ 23.32   ☽△♀ 23.51

Sunday 30th

Moon enters Capricorn 03.44

☽△☿ 06.55   ☽✶♄ 13.15

All times are GMT - add 1 hour to get BST times

July 2023

24th

Pioneer Day (Mormonism)

Mick Karn, post-punk musician and songwriter, b 1958

25th

26th

Dhamma Day (Buddhism)
Esperanto Day

27th

The BBC reported that the Loch Ness Monster did not exist, 2003

28th

World Hepatitis Day
Ashura (Islam)

Sheila Barrett, the UK's first female radio announcer, first broadcast 1933

29th

International Tiger Day

30th

International Day of Friendship

Henry Moore, sculptor, b 1898

July 2023

Monday 31st

☽△♂ 00.18   ☽△♃ 01.51   ☽△♅ 16.29   ☽✶♆ 23.55

July 2023

31st

"Before you criticise someone, you should walk a mile in their shoes. That way when you criticise them, you are a mile away and you have their shoes."

~ Jack Handey

August 2023

"Hope is optimism with a broken heart."
~ Nick Cave

Tuesday 1st

Moon enters Aquarius 03:58

○ Full Moon 18:32

☽☌♀ 02.13   ☽☍☉ 18.32   ♂△♃ 20.45

Wednesday 2nd

☽□♃ 01.38   ☿☍♄ 02.18   ☽□♅ 15.44   ☽☍♀ 21.15

Thursday 3rd

Moon enters Pisces 03:05

☽☌♄ 11.52   ☽☍☿ 15.03

Friday 4th

☽✶♃ 01.19   ☽☍♂ 03.15   ☽✶♅ 15.35   ☽☌♆ 23.00

Saturday 5th

Moon enters Aries 03:19

☽✶♀ 01.21

Sunday 6th

☽△☉ 01.40   ☽△♀ 20.35

All times are GMT - add 1 hour to get BST times

August 2023

"Always beware of somebody who is a really good listener."

~ Terry Pratchett

1st

Yorkshire Day
Lammas (Lughnasad)

Laura Knight, artist, b 1877

2nd

3rd

The Beatles performed at Liverpool's Cavern Club for the last time 1963

4th

International Beer Day

5th

6th

August 2023

Monday 7th   Moon enters Taurus 06:24

☉□♃ 01.40   ☽□♀ 04.13   ☽⚹♄ 15.46

Tuesday 8th
◐ Last Quarter 10.28

☽△☿ 05.09   ☽☌♃ 08.11   ☽□☉ 10.28   ☽△♂ 14.46   ☽☌♅ 23.50

Wednesday 9th   Moon enters Gemini 13:05

☽□♀ 00.21   ☽⚹♆ 08.00   ☽△♀ 10.39   ☽□♄ 22.45

Thursday 10th

☿△♃ 00.47   ☽□♀ 19.02   ☽⚹☉ 23.37

Friday 11th   Moon enters Cancer 22.53

☽□♂ 02.28   ☽⚹♀ 06.52   ☽□♆ 17.27

Saturday 12th

☽△♄ 08.37

Sunday 13th

☽⚹♃ 04.06   ☽⚹☿ 09.26   ☉☌♀ 11.16   ☽⚹♂ 16.56   ☽⚹♅ 20.30

All times are GMT - add 1 hour to get BST times

August 2023

7th

Bank Holiday (Ireland, Scotland only)
Commerce Day (Iceland)

8th

International Cat Day

9th

International Day of the World's Indigenous Peoples

Whitney Houston, American singer and actress, b 1963

10th

International Biodiesel Day

11th

12th

International Youth Day
Sea Org Day (Scientology)
World Elephant day

Helena Blavatsky, founder of Theosophy, b 1831

13th

International Left-Handers Day
World organ Donation Day
Bon Festival (Buddhist)

August 2023

Monday 14th

Moon enters Leo 10.36

☽△Ψ 04.57   ☽☌°♀ 07.46

Tuesday 15th

☽□♃ 16.44

Wednesday 16th
● New Moon 09:38

Moon enters Virgo 23.40

☽☌♀ 00.44   ☉□♅ 02.35   ☽□♅ 09.04   ☽☌☉ 09.38   ♂△♅ 13.53

Thursday 17th

☽☌°♄ 08.32

Friday 18th

☽△♃ 05.48   ☽☌♀ 17.09   ☽△♅ 17.51

Saturday 19th

Moon enters Libra 11.53

☽☌♂ 00.57   ☽☌°Ψ 06.01   ☽△♀ 08.51

Sunday 20th

☽⚹♀ 20.07

All times are GMT - add 1 hour to get BST times

August 2023

14th

15th **First day of Flooding of the Nile (Egypt, Coptic Church)**

16th

Roy Firebrace, sidereal astrologer, b 1889

17th

18th **Birthday of Virginia Dare (Roanoke Island)**

Carl Wayne, British rock singer and actor, b 1943

19th **World Humanitarian Day**

Marsilio Ficino, astrologer, philosopher and scholar, b 1433

20th **World Mosquito Day**

August 2023

Monday 21st

Moon enters Scorpio 23.22

Tuesday 22nd

☽□♀ 20.19   ☽⚹☉ 20.31

Wednesday 23rd

☽△♄ 01.33   ♀□♃ 12.16   ♂☌♆ 20.34

Mercury goes retrograde until 16th September
Sun enters Virgo 09.01

Thursday 24th
◐ First Quarter 09:57

☽□♀ 04.10   ☽☌♃ 04.48   ☽⚹☿ 17.03   ☽☌♅ 19.19

Moon enters Sagittarius 08.07

Friday 25th

☽△♆ 02.33   ☽⚹♂ 04.09   ☽⚹♀ 05.10   ☽□☉ 09.57   ☽□♄ 15.29

Saturday 26th

♂△♀ 00.23   ☽△♀ 09.27   ☽□☿ 22.43

Moon enters Capricorn 13.05

Sunday 27th

☽□♆ 07.49   ☽△☉ 18.39   ☽⚹♄ 19.39

Mars enters Libra 13.20

☉☌♄ 08.28   ☽△♃ 14.58

All times are GMT - add 1 hour to get BST times

August 2023

21st

22nd   **Qixi Festival (Chinese)**

23rd

Stanisław Lubieniecki, Polish astronomer, theologian, historian, b 1623
24th   **International Strange Music Day**

25th

26th

27th

August 2023

Monday 28th

Moon enters Aquarius 14.32

☽△☿ 00.00   ☽△♅ 03.22   ☽✳Ψ 09.29   ☽☌♀ 11.49   ☽△♂ 15.39

Tuesday 29th

☽☌°♀ 10.56   ☽□♃ 15.11

Wednesday 30th

Moon enters Pisces 13.56

☽□♅ 03.04   ☽☌♄ 19.33

Thursday 31st
○ Full Moon 01:36

☽☌°☉ 01.36   ☽✳♃ 14.25   ☽☌°☿ 19.28

"Gods don't like people not doing much work. People who aren't busy all the time might start to think."

- Terry Pratchett (Small Gods)

August 2023

28th   **Bank Holiday (except in Scotland)**

29th

Richard Attenborough, actor and film director, b 1923

30th   **International Day of the Disappeared**
Raksha Bandhan (Hindu)
Ghost festival (Chinese)

Mary Shelley, author of *Frankenstein*, b 1797

31st

*"While the novelist is banging away on the typewriter,
the poet is gazing at a fly on the windowpane."*

~ Billy Collins

September 2023

"As you get older, three things happen. The first is your memory goes, and I can't remember the other two."

~ Sir Norman Wisdom

Friday 1st	Moon enters Aries 13.25

☽✶♅ 02.20   ☽☌♆ 08.13   ☽✶♀ 10.36   ☽☌°♂ 18.50

Saturday 2nd

☽△♀ 09.19

Sunday 3rd	Moon enters Taurus 15.00

☽□♀ 11.57   ☽✶♄ 20.36

All times are GMT - add 1 hour to get BST times

September 2023

*"There's a theory which states that if ever anyone
discovers exactly what the Universe is for and why it is
here, it will instantly disappear and be replaced by
something even more bizarre and inexplicable.There's
another theory which states that this has already
happened."*

~ Douglas Adams

1st

Cetshwayo is anointed King of the Zulu Kingdom, 1873

2nd

René Thom, French mathematician, founder of Catastrophe Theory, b 1923

3rd

September 2023

Monday 4th

Jupiter goes retrograde until 31st December
Venus turns direct

☿△♃ 10.29 ☽△☉ 11.12 ☽□♀ 12.08 ☽△☿ 17.35 ☽☌♃ 18.06

Tuesday 5th

Moon enters Gemini 20.07

☽☌♅ 07.28 ☽✶♆ 13.59 ☽△♀ 16.46

Wednesday 6th

◖ Last Quarter 22:21

☽□♄ 01.50 ☽△♂ 07.45 ☉☌☿ 11.09 ☽✶♀ 19.06 ☽□♅ 2046 ☽□☉ 22.21

Thursday 7th

☽□♆ 22.22

Friday 8th

Moon enters Cancer 05.00

☽△♄ 10.33 ☉△♃ 11.13 ☽□♂ 20.33

Saturday 9th

☽✶♀ 02.57 ☽✶♃ 11.38 ☽✶☉ 13.49

Sunday 10th

Moon enters Leo 16.36

☽✶♅ 02.34 ☽△♆ 09.36 ☽☌♀ 12.47

All times are GMT - add 1 hour to get BST times

September 2023

4th

Google founded, 1998

5th

International Day of Charity

6th

7th

Interpol founded 1923

8th

Nativity of the Virgin Mary (Christian)
Krishna Janmashtami (Hindu)
International Literacy Day

9th

Chrysanthemum Day (Japan)
Emergency Services Day

The world's first logrolling contest was held, in Omaha,1898

10th

World Suicide Prevention Day

Marie Laveau, Creole herbalist, midwife and Voodoo practitioner, b 1801

September 2023

Monday 11th

☽✶♂ 12.06 ☽☌♀ 19.32 ☽☐♃ 23N54

Tuesday 12th

☽☐♅ 15.06

Moon enters Virgo 05.18

Wednesday 13th

☽☍♄ 10.31 ☽☌☿ 22.04

Thursday 14th

☽△♃ 12.27

Moon enters Libra 17.44

Friday 15th
● New Moon 01.40

☽☌☉ 01.40 ☽△♅ 03.37 ☽☍♆ 10.30 ☽△♀ 13.49

Saturday 16th

☉△♅ ☽☌♂ 19.53 ☽✶♀ 23.57

Sunday 17th

♀☐♃ 06.10

All times are GMT - add 1 hour to get BST times

September 2023

11th
Nayrouz (Coptic Orthodox Church)
Enkutash (Rastafari, Ethiopia, Eritrea)
Abbots Bromley Horn Dance

John Martyn, British singer, songwriter and guitarist, b 1948

12th
UN Day for South-South Co-operation

13th
Day of the Programmer
Roald Dahl Day

14th

Amy Winehouse, British soul/R&B/jazz singer, b 1983

15th
International Day of Democracy
Rosh Hashanah (Jewish)
Battle of Britain Day

The first Scottish immigrants arrived in Nova Scotia 1773

16th
International Day for the Preservation of the Ozone Layer

17th

Murry Hope, occultist, priestess, writer, b 1929

September 2023

Monday 18th	Moon enters Scorpio 04.48

☽□♀ 01.06   ☽△♄ 09.09   ☽✳☿ 21.52

Tuesday 19th

☽☌♃ 10.16   ☉☌♆ 11.17   ☽□♀ 12.29

Wednesday 20th	Moon enters Sagittarius 14.06

☽☌♅ 00.46   ☽△♆ 07.06   ☽✳☉ 08.47   ☽✳♅ 10.21   ☽□♄ 17.58

Thursday 21st

☉△♀ 05.21   ☽✳♂ 20.12   ☽△♀ 22.25

Friday 22nd ◑ First Quarter 19:32	Moon enters Capricorn 20.20

☽□♆ 13.37   ☽□☉ 19.32   ☽✳♄ 23.44

Saturday 23rd	Sun enters Libra 06:50

☽△☿ 18.24   ☽△♃ 22.12

Sunday 24th	Moon enters Aquarius 23.49

☽□♂ 03.17   ☽△♅ 11.27

All times are GMT - add 1 hour to get BST times

September 2023

18th   **World Water Monitoring Day**

19th

20th

21st   **International Day of Peace**

Dannie Abse, Welsh poet and physician, b 1923

22nd

23rd   **International Day of Sign Language**
                                      Celebrate Bisexuality Day
                                         AUTUMN EQUINOX
                                              Mabon

24th   **Yom Kippur (Jewish)**

September 2023

Monday 25th

☽△☉ 02.26 ☿△♃ 12.10 ♀□♃ 23.49

Tuesday 26th

☽△♂ 07.13 ☽☍♀ 08.47 ☽□♅ 12.39

Wednesday 27th

Moon enters Pisces 00.18

♆☽☌♄ 03.01 ☽✶♃ 23.46

Thursday 28th

Venus enters Libra 07:49

☽☍☿ 06.18 ☽✶♅ 12.35 ☽☌♆ 17.54 ☽✶♇ 20.58

Friday 29th

Moon enters Aries 00.17

◯ Full Moon 09:57

☽☍☉ 09.57 ♀□♅ 17.53

Saturday 30th

☽☍♂ 12.19 ☽△♀ 14.08 ☿△♅ 16.55 ☽□♇ 21.49

"You know you're getting old when you stoop to tie your shoelaces and wonder what else you could do while you're down there."

~ George Burns

All times are GMT - add 1 hour to get BST times

September 2023

25th

26th   European Day of Languages
                                                  Petrov Day

                         George Gershwin, American composer, b 1898
27th   Worls Tourism Day

                    Ermentrude of Orléans, Queen of the Franks, b 823
28th   World Rabies Day

                       The first issue of *Radio Times* was published 1923
29th   First day of Sukkot (Jewish)
                                           Mid-Autumn Festival (Chinese)
                                                  World Heart Day

---

30th   International Blasphemy Day

"Develop your eccentricities while you are young.
That way, when you get old, people won't think
you're going gaga."

~ David Ogilvy

October 2023

"Humans need fantasy to be human, to be the place where the falling angel meets the rising ape."

~ Terry Pratchett

Sunday 1st   Moon enters Taurus 01.18

☽⚹♄ 0345

All times are GMT - add 1 hour to get BST times

October 2023

"Whatever women do they must do twice as well as men to be thought half as good. Luckily, this is not difficult."

~ Charlotte Whitton

1st	**International Day of Older Persons** **International Coffee Day** **Lincolnshire Day**

Annie Besant, socialist, womens' rights activist and Theosophist, b 1847

October 2023

Monday 2nd

☽☌♃ 01.37 ☿☍♆ 15.34 ☽☌♅ 15.57 ☽□♀ 20.07 ☽✶♆ 21.47 ☽△☿ 22.41

Tuesday 3rd

Moon enters Gemini 05.03

☽△♀ 01.20 ☽□♄ 07.29 ☿△♀ 19.20

Wednesday 4th

☽△☉ 00.03

Thursday 5th

Mercury enters Libra 00.09
Moon enters Cancer 12.32

☽△♂ 03.32 ☽□♆ 04.37 ☽✶♀ 04.34 ☽□☿ 14.33 ☽△♄ 14.55

Friday 6th

◑ Last Quarter 13:48

☽□☉ 14.38 ☽✶♃ 15.29

Saturday 7th

Moon enters Leo 23.24

☽✶♅ 08.22 ☽△♆ 14.58 ☽□♂ 17.25 ☽☍♀ 19.12

Sunday 8th

☽✶♀ 11.47

All times are GMT - add 1 hour to get BST times

October 2023

2nd

Margaret Hone, astrologer, b 1892

3rd

Allan Kardec, founder of Spiritism, b 1804

4th

Blessing of the Animals (Christianity)
World Animal Day

5th

World Teachers Day

6th

Simchat Torah (Jewish)

7th

8th

World Post Day

Johnny Ramone, American punk rock guitarist, b 1948

October 2023

Monday 9th
Venus enters Virgo 01.11

♂□♀ 01.05 ☽□♃ 02.55 ☽✱☉ 07.07 ☽□♅ 20.36

Tuesday 10th
Moon enters Scorpio 12.02

♀☍♄ 06.11 ☽✱♂ 09.37 ☽☍♄ 14.06 ☽☌♀ 14.47

Wednesday 11th
Pluto turns direct

☽△♃ 15.06

Thursday 12th
Mars enters Scorpio 04.04

☽△♅ 09.01 ☽☍♆ 15.42 ☽△♀ 20.10

Friday 13th
Moon enters Libra 00.22

♂△♄ 12.29

Saturday 14th
● New Moon 17:55
Annular Solar Eclipse

☽☌☿ 08.58 ☽☌☉ 17.55

Sunday 15th
Moon enters Scorpio 11.04

☽□♀ 17.01 ☽△♄ 12.41 ☽☌♂ 15.35 ☽✱♀ 22.51

All times are GMT - add 1 hour to get BST times

October 2023

9th	**Milad un Nabi (Islam)**

Karl Schwarzschild, German physicist and astronomer, b 1873

10th	**World Mental Health Day** **World Porridge Day**

11th	**International Day of the Girl Child**

NASA launched Pioneer 1, its first spaceship, 1958

12th	**Crowleymas (Thelema)** **Freethought Day**

13th	

A Bear Called Paddington, the first Paddington Bear book, was published 1958

14th	**World Standards Day**

15th	**First day of Navaratri (Hindu)** **Shwmae Su'mae Day (Wales)**

October 2023

Monday 16th

$\mathcal{D}\sigma^{\circ}\mathcal{4}$ 11.31

Tuesday 17th

Moon enters Sagittarius 19.36

$\mathcal{D}\sigma^{\circ}\mathrm{\aleph}$ 05.01 $\mathcal{D}\,\Psi$ 11.20 $\mathcal{D}\!*\!\mathrm{\varphi}$ 15.44 $\mathcal{D}\sigma^{\circ}\mathrm{\hbar}$ 21.02

Wednesday 18th

$\mathcal{D}\square\mathrm{\varphi}$ 11.15

Thursday 19th

$\mathcal{D}\square\Psi$ 17.53 $\mathcal{D}\!*\!\mathrm{\varphi}$ 18.25 $\mathcal{D}\!*\!\mathrm{\odot}$ 19.02

Friday 20th

Moon enters Capricorn 01.55

$\mathcal{D}\!*\!\mathrm{\hbar}$ 03.10 $\mathrm{\hbar}\sigma\mathrm{\varphi}$ 05.38 $\mathcal{D}\!*\!\sigma'$ 11.54 $\mathcal{D}\triangle\mathrm{\varphi}$ 20.59 $\mathcal{D}\triangle\mathcal{4}$ 23.50

Saturday 21st

$\mathrm{\varphi}\square\mathrm{\varphi}$ 00.51 $\mathrm{\odot}\square\mathrm{\varphi}$ 14.09 $\mathcal{D}\triangle\mathrm{\aleph}$ 16.21 $\mathcal{D}\!*\!\Psi$ 22.17

Sunday 22nd
◐ First Quarter 03:29

Moon enters Aquarius 06.06
Mercury enters Scorpio 06.29

$\mathcal{D}\sigma\mathrm{\varphi}$ 02.33 $\mathcal{D}\square\mathrm{\odot}$ 03.29 $\mathrm{\varphi}\triangle\mathcal{4}$ 04.32 $\mathcal{D}\square\mathrm{\varphi}$ 06.00 $\mathrm{\varphi}\triangle\mathrm{\hbar}$ 16.12 $\mathcal{D}\square\sigma'$ 18.21

All times are GMT - add 1 hour to get BST times

October 2023

16th

World Food Day

17th

International Day for the Eradication of Poverty

The Great London Beer Flood (eight people drowned) 1814

18th

World Menopause Day

19th

Oxfordshire Day

The antibiotic streptomycin was first isolated, 1943

20th

International Sloth day
World Osteoporosis Day
World Statistics Day

Arthur Rimbaud, poet and surrealist, b 1854

21st

Observe the Moon Night

22nd

International Stuttering Awareness Day

Timothy Leary, psychologist and psychedelics researcher, b 1920

October 2023

Monday 23rd

Sun enters Scorpio 16:21

☽□♃ 02.27   ☽□♅ 19.04

Tuesday 24th

Moon enters Pisces 08.33

☉△♄ 07.14   ☽♂♄ 09.34   ☽△☿ 14.57   ☽△♂ 22.58

Wednesday 25th

☽✶♃ 03.57   ☽♂♀ 09.52   ☽□☿ 18.49   ☽✶♅ 20.35

Thursday 26th

Moon enters Aries 10.02

☽♂♆ 02.22   ☽✶♀ 06.39

Friday 27th

There are no major mundane aspects today

Saturday 28th
◯ Full Moon 20:24
Partial Lunar Eclipse

Moon enters Taurus 11.44

☽□♀ 08.20   ☽✶♄ 12.40   ♂♂♃ 16.03   ☽♂☉ 20.24

Sunday 29th

☿♂♃ 03.44   ☽♂♃ 06.37   ☽♂♀ 07.00   ☽♂♂ 07.30   ☿♂♂ 14.22   ☽△♀ 21.33

All times are GMT - add 1 hour to get BST times

October 2023

23rd   **Double Ninth Festival (Chinese)**
                                                              Mole Day

24th   **World Polio Day**
                                                  United Nations Day

25th

26th

27th   **World day For Audiovisual Heritage**

                        Roy Lichtenstein, American Pop artist, b 1923
28th

29th   **End of British Summer Time (clocks go back)**

October 2022

Monday 30th

Moon enters Gemini 15.08

☽☌♅ 00.36   ☽✶♆ 06.50   ☽△♀ 11.36   ☽□♄ 16.03

Tuesday 31st

♀△♅ 12.51

"There isn't a way things should be. There is only what happens, and what we do."

~ Terry Pratchett (A Hatful of Sky)

October 2022

30th

31st

All Hallows Eve (Christian)
Samhain Eve (Pagan)

"Legs are hereditary, and run in most families."
~ Spike Milligan

November 2023

"The true meaning of life is to plant trees,
under whose shade you do not expect to sit."

~ Anonymous

Wednesday 1st

Moon enters Cancer 21.30

☽□♀ 07.26   ☽□♆ 12.46   ☽□♄ 22.29

Thursday 2nd

☽△☉ 16.23   ☽✳♃ 17.31

Friday 3rd

☽△♂ 02.01   ☉☌♃ 05.02   ☽△☿ 10.49   ☽✳♅ 14.36   ☽✳♀ 21.49   ☽△♆ 21.50   ♀☌♆ 22.06

Saturday 4th

Moon enters Leo 07.21
Saturn goes direct

☽□♃ 03.46   ☽□☉ 08.37   ☽□♂ 17.00

Sunday 5th
◑ Last Quarter 08:37

☽✳♄ 08.44   ☽✳♂ 20.30   ☽□♀ 22.30

All times are GMT

November 2023

"In three words, I can sum up everything I've learned about life: it goes on."

~ Robert Frost

1st

El Dia de los Muertos (Mexico)
All Saints Day (Christian)
World Vegan Day
Samhain

The European Court of Human Rights founded 1963

2nd

All Souls Day (Catholic)

3rd

4th

Lena Zavaroni, Scottish singer and TV presenter, b 1963

5th

November 2023

Monday 6th	Moon enters Virgo 19.39

☽□♅ 02.11   ☽□☿ 07.25   ♀△♀ 14.38   ☽☌♄ 20.42

Tuesday 7th	

☿△♆ 01.37   ☿△♃ 15.43

Wednesday 8th	Venus enters Libra 09.30

☽✶☉ 02.54   ☽✶♂ 09.29   ☽△♅ 14.40   ☽☌♆ 22.40

Thursday 9th	Moon enters Libra 08.08

☿✶♀ 00.17   ☽△♀ 04.20   ☽✶☿ 04.55   ☽☌♀ 10.23

Friday 10th	Mercury enters Sagittarius 06.25

☿□♄ 15.07

Saturday 11th	Moon enters Scorpio 18.39

☽□♀ 15/05   ☽△♄ 19.43   ♂☌♅ 21.11

Sunday 12th	

☽☌♃ 12.09

All times are GMT

November 2023

6th

7th   **International Inuit Day**

8th   **World Urbanism Day**

9th

Capital punishment for all offences abolished in the UK 1998

10th

11th

12th   **World Pneumonia Day**
                                                  Diwali (Hindu)

Errol Brown, soul/funk/disco singer, b 1943

November 2023

Monday 13th
● New Moon 09:27

☽☌☉ 09.27 ☽☌♅ 10.05 ☽☌♂ 12.18 ☽△♆ 17.20 ☉☍♅ 17.21 ☽⚹♀ 23.03

Tuesday 14th
Moon enters Sagittarius 02.23

☽□♄ 03.28 ☽☌☿ 14.04 ☽⚹♀ 14.45

Wednesday 15th

☿⚹♀ 12.48 ☽□♆ 22.57

Thursday 16th

☽⚹♄ 08.49 ☽△♃ 22.48

Friday 17th

☽□♀ 00.16 ♂△♆ 08.36 ☉△♆ 14.52 ☽△♅ 19.51

Saturday 18th
Moon enters Aquarius 11.27

☽⚹♆ 02.52 ☽□☉ 03.49 ☉☌♂ 05.42 ☽☌♀ 08.27

Sunday 19th

☽⚹♃ 01.50 ☽△♀ 08.12 ☽⚹☿ 10.39 ☽□♅ 22.53

All times are GMT

November 2023

13th   **World Kindness Day**

14th   **World Diabetes Day**

15th

Nye Bevan, the politician who helped to establish the NHS, b 1897

16th   **International Day for Tolerance**

Terence McKennam mystic and ethnobotanist, b 1946

17th   **International Students' Day**

Budapest founded 1873

18th

Alan Moore, comic-book writer, artist and illustrator, b 1053

19th   **International Mens Day**
                                                  World Toilet Day

November 2023

Monday 20th ◗ First Quarter 10:50	Moon enters Pisces 14.29

☽□♂ 09.48   ☽□☉ 10.50   ☽♂♄ 15.45   ☉∗♀ 21.26

Tuesday 21st

☽∗♃ 04.20   ☽□☿ 19.16

Wednesday 22nd

Sun enters Sagittarius 14.03
Moon enters Aries 17.19

♂∗♀ 01N18   ☽♂♆ 08.45   ☽∗♀ 14.29   ☽△♂ 15.10   ☽△☉ 17.35

Thursday 23rd

☉□♄ 09.47   ☽♂♀ 22.57

Friday 24th

Mars enters Sagittarius 10.15
Moon enters Taurus 20.29

☽△☿ 03.52   ☽□♀ 17.40   ☽∗♄ 21.59

Saturday 25th

☽♂♃ 09.43   ♂□♄ 16.57

Sunday 26th

☽♂♅ 08.03   ☽∗♆ 15.42   ☽△♀ 21.52

All times are GMT

November 2023

20th

21st

Nadine Gordimer, novelist and playwright, b 1923

World Television Day

22nd

Rene Magritte, Belgian surrealistic artist, b 1898

23rd

24th

First episode of Doctor Who broadcast 1963

Evolution Day

25th

International Day for the Elimination of Violence Against Women

26th

Pat Phoenix, British actress, b 1923

November 2023

Monday 27th
◯ Full Moon 09:16

Moon enters Gemini 00.40

☽□♄ 02.22   ☽☌♂ 04.08   ☽☌☉ 09.16   ☿□♆ 13.27

Tuesday 28th

☽△♀ 17.54   ☽□♆ 21.30

Moon enters Cancer 06.54

Wednesday 29th

☽☌☿ 01.03   ☽△♄ 08.51   ☽⚹♃ 20.21

Thursday 30th

☽⚹♅ 21.20

"A computer once beat me at chess, but it
was no match for me at kick boxing."

~ Emo Philips

All times are GMT

November 2023

27th   **Lancashire Day**

28th   **Loy Krathong (Buddhist)**
                                          Bedfordshire Day

29th

CS Lewis, novelist and theologian, b 1898

30th   **Bank Holiday (Scotland only)**
                                          St Andrews Day

"There are a whole lot of people who die at
fifty and aren't buried until they are eighty."

~ Anonymous

December 2023

"Life is pleasant. Death is peaceful. It's the transition that's troublesome."

~ Isaac Asimov

Friday 1st   Mercury enters Capricorn 14.31
                                  Moon enters Leo 16.00

☽△♆ 06.04   ☽□♀ 08.09   ☽☌♀ 13.07

Saturday 2nd

☽△♂ 02.48   ☽□♃ 05.44   ☽△☉ 11.45   ☿✳♄ 15.27

Sunday 3rd

☽□♅ 08.13   ♀□♀ 13.29

All times are GMT

December 2023

"Religion is regarded by the common people as true, by the wise as false, and by the rulers as useful."

~ Seneca

1st	**World AIDS Day**

Franz Bardon, Czech occultist and teacher of Hermetics, b 1909

2nd

Maria Callas, Greek operatic soprano, b 1923

3rd	**International Day of Persons with Disabilities**

December 2023

Monday 4th

Moon enters Virgo 03.50

☽✶♀ 02.11   ☽☌°♄ 06.23   ☽△☿ 10.12   ☽△♃ 17N32   ☽□♂ 18.52

Tuesday 5th

◗ Last Quarter 05:49

☽□☉ 05.49   ☽△♅ 20.45   ♀△♄ 22.51

Wednesday 6th

Moon enters Libra 16.35
Neptune goes direct

☽☌°♆ 06.17   ☽△♀ 13.15

Thursday 7th

☽□☿ 04.00   ☽✶♂ 11.16   ☽✶☉ 23.37

Friday 8th

♀△♃ 04.09

Saturday 9th

Moon enters Scorpio 03.35

☽□♀ 01.05   ☽△♄ 06.33   ☽☌♀ 14.24   ☽☌°♃ 15.41   ☽✶☿ 17.46

Sunday 10th

♀☌°♃ 03.35   ☽☌°♅ 17.03

All times are GMT

December 2023

4th

5th

World Soil Day

Britain's first motorway, the Preston Bypass, was officially opened 1958

6th

Dion Fortune, occultist, ceremonial magician, novelist and writer, b 1890

7th

First Day of Chanukah (Jewish)

8th

Bodhi Day (Buddhist)

Jim Morrison, American rock singer, songwriter and poet, b 1943

9th

International Anti-Corruption Day
Anna's Day (Scandinavia)

10th

Human Rights Day

December 2023

Monday 11th	Moon enters Sagittarius 11.11

☽△♆ 01.58   ☽✳♀ 08.57   ☽□♄ 14.13   ☿✳♀ 19.17

Tuesday 12th
● New Moon 23:32

☽♂♂ 10.05   ☽♂☉ 23.32

Wednesday 13th
Mercury goes retrograde until 1ˢᵗ January
Moon enters Capricorn 15.31

☽□♆ 06.48   ☽✳♄ 18.39

Thursday 14th

☽△♃ 01.51   ☽♂☿ 05.47   ☽✳♀ 10.55
Moon enters Aquarius 17.56

Friday 15th

☽△♅ 01.00   ☽✳♆ 09.27   ☽♂♀ 16.04

Saturday 16th

☽□♃ 03.52   ☽□♀ 17.33   ✳♂ 20.52
Moon enters Pisces 19.58

Sunday 17th

☽□♅ 02.53   ☉□♆ 03.43   ☽✳☉ 12.04   ☽♂♄ 23.32

All times are GMT

December 2023

11th

International Mountain Day

12th

St Lucia Day (Scandinavia)

Olivia Barclay, astrologer, b 1919

13th

14th

Forty-seven Ronin Day (Tokyo)
Monkey Day

15th

Zamenhof Day (International Esperanto Community)

16th

First day of Posadas Navidena (Hispanic Christian)

17th

Dave Dee, British pop/rock singer, songwriter and musician, b 1943

December 2023

Monday 18th

☽✶♃ 05.49 ☽✶☿ 06.21 ☿△♃ 14.28

Moon enters Aries 22.47

Tuesday 19th

◖ First Quarter 18:39

☽△♀ 00.30 ☽□♂ 01.58 ☽✶♅ 05.14 ☽♂♆ 14.07 ☽□☉ 18.39 ☽✶♀ 21.03

Wednesday 20th

☽□☿ 05.42

Thursday 21st

♀♂♅ 07.04 ☽△♂ 08.23 ☿✶♄ 12.33

Moon enters Taurus 02.50

Sun enters Capricorn 03.27

Friday 22nd

☽□♀ 01.11 ☽△☉ 02.47 ☽△☿ 05.21 ☽✶♄ 07.08 ☽♂♃ 12.53 ☉♂☿ 18.54

Mercury enters Sagittarius 06.17

Saturday 23rd

☽♂♅ 13.33 ☽♂♀ 19.04 ☽✶♆ 23.12

Moon enters Gemini 08.15

Sunday 24th

☽△♀ 06.40 ☽□♄ 12.58 ☉✶♄ 17.28

All times are GMT

December 2023

18th

19th   International Migrants Day
                                            Arabic Language Day

---

20th   International Human Solidarity Day

21st   Ziemassvētki (Latvia)

Frank Zappa, US rock/avant-garde/jazz composer and guitarist, b 1940

22nd   WINTER SOLSTICE
                                          Dongzhi Festival (East Asia)
                                                         Yule

---

23rd   Night of the Radishes (Oaxaca City, Mexico)
                                      HumanLight (Secular Humanism)

First case of 'mad cow disease' (BSE) discovered 2003

24th   Christmas Eve (Christian)

Caroline Aherne, British comedian, writer and television actress, b 1963

December 2023

Monday 25th

♀△♆ 17.15

Tuesday 26th

Moon enters Cancer 15.15

☽☍♂ 02.08 ☽□♆ 05.57 ☽☍☿ 07.55 ☽△♄ 20.30

Wednesday 27th

◯ Full Moon 00:33

☽☍☉ 00.23 ☽✶♃ 01.45 ☽□♆ 07.43 ☉△♃ 15.28

Thursday 28th

☿☌♂ 00.31 ☽✶♅ 04.04 ☽△♆ 14.45 ☽△♀ 22.12 ♂□♆ 22.16 ☽☍♀ 22.57

Friday 29th

Moon enters Leo 00.23
Venus enters Sagittarius 20.24

♀✶♀ 06.01 ☽□♃ 11.17

Saturday 30th

☽□♅ 14.39 ☽△☿ 21.00

Sunday 31st

Moon enters Virgo 11.53
Jupiter goes direct

☽△♂ 05.18 ☽□♀ 16.23 ☽☍♄ 18.24 ☽△♃ 23.10

All times are GMT

December 2023

25th

Malkh-Festival (Nakh peoples of Chechnya)
Christmas Day (Christian)
Bank Holiday

St Francis of Assisi created the first Nativity Scene, in Italy, 1223

26th

Zartosht No-Diso (Zoroastrian)
Boxing Day
Bank Holiday

27th

28th

Comet Kohoutek reached perihelion (came closest to the sun), 1973

29th

The Akkala Sami language died out when its last native speaker died, 2003

30th

31st

Hogmanay

Monica Sjöö, artist, writer, Pagan activist and eco-feminist, b 1938

THE PSYCHIC GUIDE
A - Z

Acupuncture A form of alternative medicine that involves thin needles being pushed into the skin along 'meridian lines'. This is said to restore the body's energy balance; many practitioners claim that is is most useful in relieving pain. However, numerous studies have shown very little effect.

Afterlife Primitive humans believed in an afterlife over half a million years ago. Ancient peoples (100,000 years ago) had their belongings and animals buried with them to provide for themselves in the next life.

Akashic Record A kind of cosmic memory bank in which everything that ever happened is said to be recorded. Each individual soul imprints its own record on time and space. Akashic is a Sanskrit word meaning fundamental, etheric substance of the universe.

Alchemy The medieval science where the practitioner is involved in the transmutation and transformation of base metals such as lead into gold. It is also the search for the philosopher's stone, or the elixir of life (which is now considered to be what the ancient Alchemists were searching for) and evolution to a higher level of ability and development. The transmutation of base metal into gold symbolised the transformation of material and natural man into spiritual man. Each person belongs to both the spiritual and material world and contains a spark of the universal spirit imprisoned in matter, which the Alchemist strives to set free.

Almagest An astronomical work in thirteen volumes written by Ptolemy the Alexandrian astronomer around AD 200.

Alpha Centauri A triple star system containing the nearest stars to our sun. They are in the constellation of Centaurus - Chiron the Centaur, tutor to Jason and Hercules.

Amulets and Talismans Amulets are usually worn as charms and are thought of as lucky and protective. An amulet guards its wearer against evil, misfortune and bad luck and they usually come in the form of a piece of jewellery. A talisman doesn't need to be worn and it incorporates symbols to represent a force or forces being called upon to gain a particular end. Talismans are made out of many different materials such as parchment, wood, stone or metal. They are charged with power and sometimes buried as part of the ritual or destroyed to release their power into the world. The thing that makes a talisman or amulet work is the belief that is put into the making and charging of them; a connection is made between your inner and outer thoughts and as the energy flows between the two it charges the amulet or talisman to enable it to do what you wish.

Anthroposophy Rudolf Steiner 1861-1925, founded the Anthroposophical Society in 1912 (*anthropos* - man, *sophia* - wisdom, in Greek). He said "Anthroposophy has its roots in the perceptions - already gained - into the spiritual world. Yet these are no more than its roots. The branches, leaves, blossoms and fruits of Anthroposophy grow into all the fields of human life and action." He developed new forms of medicine, architecture, agriculture and education, and in his early forties wrote four mystery plays about the karmic connections of a group of people in successive incarnations.

Apport An object or substance materialised from the astral plane by a medium.

Aromatherapy Aromatherapy is the use of essential oils in an unscented carrier oil to enhance the physical or emotional well-being of an individual. It originates from Egypt and all the individual odours are aligned with the planets. The oils can be used in massage, as a bath oil or in a vaporiser to fragrance a room. Because essential oils are highly concentrated it is not recommended that they be used undiluted on the skin or internally. Essential oils should NOT be administered to pregnant women and infants unless this course of action has been recommended by a competent practitioner.

Sun Frankincense, cloves, canomile, rosemary. For self-confidence, friendship and vitality.

Moon Nutmeg, jasmine, camphor. Increases sensuality.

Mercury Lavender, oregano, fennel. For intellectual powers and communication.

Venus Sandalwood, Rose, Thyme. For attracting love.

Mars Pine, geranium. For strength and determination.

Jupiter Sage. For success, wealth and luck.

Saturn Caraway, cypress. For status, self knowledge and contentment in the house.

Asteroids   Irregular pieces of rock orbiting the Sun and thought to be leftovers from the formation of the Solar System. Most of them are in the Asteroid Belt between Mars and Jupiter.

Astral Body   At night when we are asleep our soul transfers from our physical body to our astral body and rests. Our astral body is attached to our physical form by a silver cord which is very fine and supple, stretching to allow us to travel anywhere we wish in the astral regions. The astral body is a replica of our own body, although with practice any physical characteristic except eyes can be altered. The same thing happens when we die. We travel in the astral regions, but this time the transfer is permanent; the cord holding the astral body to the physical body simply dissolves. This dissolving of the cord takes place about three days after death. When it has faded, the astral body is free to go to the level it has reached in its lifetime with the knowledge it has acquired.

Astral Projection It is said by some that your astral body can travel through the astral regions at will; you can talk to people who have died, or to other people who are also alive and on earth and exploring the astral levels. It is a matter of willpower (as everything else is) and you can will yourself to astrally project by visualisation and imagination. If you can do this, your soul simply leaves your body and floats off into the astral regions, always attached to your physical body by a thin silver cord so that it doesn't get lost or detached from its other self. The cord only dissolves when there is no life force left in the physical body and it dies.

Astral Regions The astral regions are said to be where your thoughts turn into reality and your imagination can create or destroy any scenario or replica of things. These regions are made of the thoughts and feelings that have amassed in the atmosphere since time began and have formed a spiritual cloak in the air. The astral regions are like seven bands of colour dissolving into one another like a rainbow. The lower astral levels have all the unhappy, clinging, nasty, naughty, negative thoughts and these often form into a selfish energy form rather like creatures of the underworld or of nightmare. Such things rely on our fear to feed them, so they cannot harm us unless we have fear in us. Most people pass through these regions, but if we have any like feelings to these creatures we are drawn to them.

The upper four layers are created of more meritable thoughts. The fourth level is the place where people who have died and are resting go until they are ready to move on to the next part of their journey to the spirit planes.

The fifth level is the region where intellectual and artistic activity coming from the earth settles and many creative people tap into this level for inspiration.

The sixth level is where heroes play out the victories they have had on earth. Many people stay there playing and replaying situations in order to understand the good they produced.

The seventh level is made up of all the religious and mystical knowledge. The great religious minds that have travelled the earth are to be found here; this region would be known as heaven to the Christian, as paradise to the Muslim and Nirvana to the Buddhist.

Beyond all this are the mental and spiritual regions which can only be reached when we are at complete harmony with ourselves and our surroundings.

Atlantis An island or continent which is supposed to have existed in the North Atlantic Ocean. The only real reference to it was made by Plato around 350 BC, and he had only hearsay evidence of Atlantis from legend (possibly Egyptian). The island of Thira, known today as Santorini, is possibly the inspiration for the legend, due to the fact that shortly after its violent volcanic destruction the Minoan civilisation, of which it was the centre, collapsed; there are 200 known sunken cities in the Mediterranean. A theory, popular in the 19th and early 20th centuries, was that Atlantis was so far advanced technologically that the Atlanteans were able to increase their vibratory rate, so the entire civilisation vanished into a higher frequency level of existence; therefore Atlantis still exists in a parallel universe from which UFOs originate, monitoring man's progress.

Atom The atom is a basic unit of matter that consists of a dense, central nucleus surrounded by a cloud of negatively charged electrons. The name comes from the Greek word *atomos* meaning 'indivisible'.

Atomism is the concept of tiny indivisible units of matter that form the basis of everything and which exist in a void, as opposed to the philosophy that all matter is contiguous and without voids. It was first proposed by the early philosophers of both Greece and India.

Aura The aura is said to be an electromagnetic field of psychic energy varying in width and colour depending on the spiritual and physical state of the person or thing. In 1911, a physician named Walter J. Kilner put a dilute solution of dye between two glass plates. He claimed that 95% of those who tried (under his supervision) saw the human aura through these plates. He observed that one person could project auric rods from her body, so this could be the way psychokinesis might work. Everything has an aura, including plants, animals and minerals. The aura can allegedly be photographed, but only by using special photography equipment - see the entry for **Kirlian photography**.

Aurora The phenomenon caused by the impact of solar particles on earth's upper atmosphere, usually at the poles. Another name for the Aurora is Northern Lights.

Automatic Writing Writing done by a medium when in trance originating from the spirit world, not consciously produced. The handwriting style is invariably totally different from the medium's own. William Blake, the poet and artist, claimed that most of his poetry was dictated to him by dead poets and his paintings were visions he was guided to produce.

Aztecs The Aztecs were a nomadic tribe of people who settled in central America (now Mexico) about 500 years ago. Other peoples and civilisations had lived in this region before the Aztecs. The Toltecs had built great cities but these had been destroyed before the Aztecs arrived. The Chichemecs (or barbarians) lived to the north and the Maya in the area that now consists of Guatemala, Belize, Honduras, Nicaragua, and part of Costa Rica. The Aztecs had an unusual 260-day calendar to calculate the dates of religious festivals; their astronomers had also worked out the 365-day solar calendar as well. Every 52 years, these two calendars coincided, and the Aztecs performed a ceremony to celebrate another 52 years of life. The Aztecs believed that human sacrifice was a fair exchange for the sacrifices that the Gods had made to create the earth and humanity. The Gods were offered these sacrifices so that the sun would rise every day and that mankind would live. These human sacrifices would first be drugged with a sacred drink, then their hearts would be cut out and offered up to the sun god. They also sacrificed dogs and turkeys to their gods. They had very fierce-looking gods and life was harsh for them - they were at the mercy of wild animals, famine and floods. Their capital city, Tenochtitlán, was constructed of mud bricks and stone and took 200 years to build. They were ruled by a king and used canals as trade and travel routes instead of roads.

They do not appear to have used money and it is thought they used barter and exchange to obtain goods. They had large markets where food, precious metals, feathers (used for cloaks and as religious symbols), jade, cocoa beans, slaves (captured from wars with neighbouring tribes) and various types of honey were available. When the Spanish explorer Cortés landed in Mexico in 1519, the Aztec king Montezuma welcomed him and his men, thinking that these white men could possibly be one of their gods (who had white skin and red hair and whose return had been prophesied) returning to the land. The Spaniards eventually killed the Aztecs for their gold and land; 100,000 died in battle and many more were killed by chicken pox, venereal disease and other infections bought by the Spanish, thus ending the Aztec empire. Most of the golden ornaments of the Aztecs were melted down; many of the temples were torn down by the Spanish priests, who also destroyed most of the Codices - sacred manuscripts made of deer hide or pounded bark, painted on both sides and folded. Very few of those have survived.

Ba Egyptian name for the Soul, which was said to roam burial places.

Bahá'í The Bahá'í Faith was founded in 19th-century Persia by a spiritual teacher called Bahá'u'lláh and nowadays has over six million followers worldwide. The tenets of this religion are that humanity is one single race that will be unified into a peaceful global society; and that there is only one God who has communicated with mankind via a series of divine messengers. These messengers have included all the founders and teachers of previous religions, including Jesus, Mohammed and the Buddha. Thus all religions and races are one, in the teachings, and religious fundamentalism is specifically forbidden.

Belief This is conviction based on non-verifiable grounds, about the truth or reality of something. Belief accepts an alleged fact as correct or true without positive proof or knowledge.

Bilocation The power to appear in two places at once; or the phenomenon of seeing an astral or psychic double. This is said to occur when a person is on the brink of death, when their presence can be witnessed by a loved one many miles away.

Biorhythms The theory of biorhythms assumes that man has three biological cycles which began at birth and continue until death. They are of fixed length though it may be that individual experience of the peaks and troughs will vary widely. The three cycles are the physical (23 days), the mental (33 days) and the emotional (28 days).

Blue Moon "Once in a blue Moon" is a term applied to something that happens very infrequently. It's also an astronomical term. There are four astronomical 'seasons' in a year; a 'season' runs from a solstice or an equinox to the following equinox or solstice (from the Midwinter Solstice to the Spring Equinox, for example). There are usually three Full Moons in such a season, but very occasionally four; a 'Blue Moon' is the third of the four Full Moons. The name is also sometimes applied to the second Full Moon that occurs in a calendar month. It is not really known why it should be called a 'Blue' Moon; the most popular explanation is that such Moons were printed in blue instead of red in almanacs.

Books of the Dead *The Egyptian Book of the Dead:* Ancient Egyptian texts from about 16thC BC and earlier. They deal with life in the afterworld, containing invocations to be spoken by the deceased. These papyri were buried with the mummified corpse and were a guarantee of protection in the afterlife. Texts from various tombs have been compiled to make a modern "The Egyptian Book of the Dead".

The Tibetan Book of the Dead: Also known as the *Bardo Thodol*, this was written as a book, concerned with the journey of the soul after death. It describes the three stages of the after-death journey - joy at loss of self, visions (both good and bad) and rebirth into the physical world. It is also a book of teachings for the living, describing the formation of the world out of the five elements.

Brainwaves Weak electrical impulses from the brain which can be recorded graphically. The range of *Beta* brainwaves are greatest when there is more concentration or mental effort, 13 to 26 cycles per second. *Alpha* brainwaves go between 8 and 12 cycles per second and occur when we are in a state of relaxed awareness, usually disappearing when our attention is stimulated. *Theta,* 4 to 7 cycles, produce a deep meditative state. *Delta,* below 4 cycles, are associated with deep sleep.

Caduceus A Latin word for a herald's staff. It is a wand with wings at the top and two snakes entwined around it. Hermes, the Greek God carries one. In alchemy it is a symbol representing the uniting of opposites but more generally it is interpreted as an emblem of power (the wand), and wisdom (the snakes). It is also a symbol of healing.

Candlemass In America, the 2nd of February is Groundhog Day; if a groundhog can see his own shadow on this day, the winter will remain for another six weeks. In the Christian calendar it is the feast of Candlemas, when Jesus was presented at the temple in Jerusalem. In English tradition, lighted candles were carried in procession; the name derives from this. The weather on Candlemas Day may truly indicate what is to come; if anti-cyclonic conditions are established, skies may well be clear and such conditions often persist for a couple of weeks.

Carbon Cycle This is the biogeochemical cycle by which carbon is exchanged among the animals, plants, lands, seas and atmosphere of the Earth. It is one of the most important cycles of the earth and allows for carbon to be recycled and reused throughout the biosphere and all of its organisms. Carbon is essential to earth life and ultimately we are all made of immortal carbon atoms that have been circulating since the beginning of time.

Cayce, Edgar (1877 - 1945) An American psychic. One of the most documented psychics of the 20th century, he left more than 14,000 of his writings which he gave whilst in a self induced trance state. He was said to have been accurate in diagnosing illnesses whilst in trance. He founded the Association for Research and Enlightenment (A.R.E.) in 1931. Thousands of people now attend the conferences and workshops in Virginia Beach, Virginia, USA. The library there contains one of the largest parapsychological collections in the world - over 70,000 volumes - and an online database of Cayce's readings can be accessed by members on their website.

Chakras These are energy centres in the body, where the energy from the cosmos can be drawn in giving life to the body and power to the psyche. There are seven main chakras situated the base of the spine, belly, solar plexus, heart, throat, third eye and crown of head.

Chaos Theory Chaos theory is science attempting to explain the predictable randomness which exists in the universe, from the movement of the moons and planets to weather patterns on earth. Variations which are too small to measure can have an enormous and unforeseen effect. It is said that the movement of a butterfly's wing can affect the weather on the other side of the world. Chaos theory looks at science on a human scale. Mathematics is used to look at chaos in nature - fractals - computer simulations from insoluble mathematical equations which suggest, due to the endlessly moving patterns, that time makes creativity possible. The term 'fractals' was invented by a mathematician called Benoit Mandelbrot in 1975. The patterns created are due to a self repeating motif which occurs at smaller scales *ad infinitum*. A simple mathematical formula can produce beautiful patterns when repeated over and over again. Fractal patterns occur in nature in the pattern of a snowflake.

China This country has been an empire from very early times. It had magical organisations similar to ancient Egypt, with a priest-ruler called the Wang who was responsible for the harvest and the general welfare of the people. The earliest recorded dynasty is the *Hsia* dynasty from 2205 BC to 1766 BC. It was not until the *Chun* dynasty in 226 BC that the country was called China or Tsina. The Great Wall was built to keep out the Mongolian invaders. The country was divided into 36 provinces, corresponding to the 36 decanates of the Heavenly Sphere (the earth had to correspond to the heavens).

Chinese Coins In ancient China the name for money, Qian, was once the name of a farming tool which was used for exchange. Thus the earliest coins were made to look like farming implements (shovels, knives etc.) with decorative words carved on them. It is believed that ancient coins can banish evil spirits.

Chinese Elements There are five elements or perpetually active principles of nature, upon which the whole scheme of Chinese philosophy is based.

Water - produces Wood but destroys Fire

Fire - produces Earth but destroys Metal

Metal - produces Water but destroys Wood

Wood - produces Fire but destroys Earth

Earth - produces Metal but destroys Water

Chinese Imperial Encyclopaedia The Ku-Chin T'u-Shu Chi-Ch'eng. The all-embracing illustrated volume of all things then and now. It was begun in the mid-18th century and was intended to be a record of all human knowledge. When completed, it had over 10,000 volumes - 40 of which were for the index alone. There were probably no more than thirty copies printed. Today there is only one copy outside Chine, in the British Library. As each section of the encyclopaedia was printed, the metal printing blocks were then melted down to make coins.

Chinese New Year The main Festival of the Chinese calendar which occurs on the second new moon after the winter solstice. It is considered unlucky to use scissors or knives on New Year's day. Red packets containing money are given as gifts to each other by friends. As part of the celebrations, firecrackers are lit to ward off evil spirits. From January 22nd 2023 to February 10th 2024 it is the Year of the Rabbit.

The **Church of All Worlds** was the first Pagan Church to be officially recognised in the United States, in March 1968. It was founded by Oberon Zell, who had been inspired by reading about the concept of Nests - communities that worked and lived together for the purpose of spiritual development - in Robert Heinlein's *Stranger In A Strange Land.* CAW members practice a wide range of magikal, occult and Earth-based beliefs; the only rule is to commit to "a way of life that is ethical, benevolent, humanistic, life-affirming, ecstatic and ecologically sane." Their website can be found at caw.org.

Church of the SubGenius This is a 'parody religion', founded in the 1970s in the US. Purportedly based on the teachings and life of a salesman named JR "Bob" Dobbs, their supreme deity is named Jehovah 1; followers also worship a number of lesser deities drawn from all the world's religions; they practice "slack", which is basically the avoidance of hard work. Essentially, the Church's underlying purpose is to satirise established religion. It has been compared to **Discordianism**.

Clairaudience This is the ability to hear things said to you in your mind by dwellers on the astral planes. We all have the ability to listen and hear and ask for guidance or answers; the trick is to learn to listen to what is being said to you, by stilling your mind and concentrating.

Clairvoyance Clairvoyance means 'clear sight'. It is claimed that we all have powers inside us that can be called clairvoyance or ESP. As the ability to use these comes from deep inside us, its strength depends upon our spiritual development. Clairvoyance is used for seeing spirit guides and spirit forms of people who have died, and for communicating with them. To be clairvoyant, one has to learn to open the third eye. This is between the eyebrows and is in some way connected to the pineal gland in the middle of the brain. As we become more psychically developed, the veils covering the third eye dissolve until it is fully open. Clairvoyants can open and shut this eye as they need, to perceive. Clairvoyance means you see into the past or future in your mind's eye or imagination. There are many ways of looking into the future and the past - tarot cards, tea leaves, crystal balls, palmistry, but all of these are merely an aid to the clairvoyant's ability.

Coincidences are sign posts to the senses to indicate that you are on the correct path.

Colour Meanings White - unity; Grey - privacy; Brown - practicality; Pink - frustration; Violet - leadership; Blue - inspiration; Green- individualism; Yellow - spirituality; Red - risk; Black - denial

Comets These are celestial bodies composed of dust and ice, orbiting in and around the Solar System. (They should not be confused with asteroids, which are solid rocky bodies.) They mainly form in the outer reaches of the Solar System, well beyond Neptune in a zone known as the Kuiper Belt.

Although some comets have orbital periods of hundreds of thousands of years, most are relatively short-lived, sometimes lasting only a few centuries before they break up. Another thing that distinguishes them from asteroids is the spectacular tail that a comet develops when it enters the inner Solar System. This is formed by ice that is blasted off the comet's body by the Solar wind emanating from the Sun.

Confucius Confucius lived from 551-479 BC, reaching the age of 73. He was one of China's greatest sages. He taught that the nature of man is pure at birth and becomes stained only by the impurity of its surroundings. There were Confucian temples in every Chinese towns until the Communist Revolution. Official worship of Confucius was carried out at the Spring and Autumn equinoxes. He is addressed as '*Honoured of Heaven who causes literature to flourish and the world to prosper*'. The ethics of Confucianism are based on the following concepts:

1) The Universe is regulated by an order which is moral in its essence.

2) Man is morally good by nature and it is up to him to remain so.

3) The individual must rectify himself before he can rectify others. He must study the teachings of the Ancients.

4) Above all, it is essential to cultivate the five Virtues: Benevolence, Justice, Propriety, Wisdom and Sincerity.

Cosmology The study of the whole universe, its structure, origin, evolution and final state.

Crystals Crystals are formed in cavities or hollows in the earth's surface and grow from natural solutions in a fixed pattern which varies with crystal type. Quartz is one of the more commonly found minerals. 12.5% of the Earth's crust consists of silicic acid. The Earth's crust is a web of quartz, but only a very small percentage of this is crystalline, where perfect conditions prevail. The word crystal (in Greek *krystallos)* means frozen in suspension. Scientists looking into the atomic structure of crystals find, as well as the perfect order, a lively exchange of electrons and electromagnetic energies among grid positions. Rock crystal contains a fine network of double helix spirals of silicon-oxygen tetrahedrons. These spirals possess a fine elasticity, which, when compressed, produce a flow of electricity. The energy field or aura produced by a person interacts with the pattern of the crystal and causes it to respond to human energy. All crystals must be cleansed before use. Wash carefully in running water, then place the crystal in a bowl containing one teaspoon of sea salt dissolved in one pint of water and leave for 24 hours, remove from salt water, rinse with running water and allow to dry naturally in sunlight.

Curses A curse is the intention of a very strongly formed thought to do evil. It is projected out of the mind of a person towards the person it is intended to harm. People can be put under a great deal of emotional pressure if they know they have been cursed. This may cause their disease-fighting immune system to collapse, making them ill, in the same way that a positive mental outlook can aid recovery from diseases.

Cycle of Sixty Also known as the Sexagenary cycle, this is a Chinese calendrical system of signs or characters (known as the Ten Celestial Stems with Twelve Celestial Branches) organised into a 60-year cycle. It has been found in the earliest written records in China - 1250BC - and almost certainly predates them. A method of recording days and lunar months, it was only sometime around 350BC that it was adapted to record years also.

Daimon In Greek mythology, a divinity which advised and informed the one it served.

Death The soul simply floats away when the energy inside the physical body dies, either through natural ageing, malfunction or accident. Then the thin cord holding our physical body to our astral body shrivels up and disappears, leaving our astral body free to travel on without any more physical pain or suffering. Heaven and Hell are here on Earth, we make our own Heaven and Hell by the way we live our lives.

Déjà-vu This can be a past-life memory, unconscious memories of a dream, or the two hemispheres of the brain operating slightly 'out of sync'.

Dervishes These are a **Sufi** sect whose twirling rituals symbolise the rotation of the universe and induce a state of trance in which they claim a direct link with God.

Discordianism is a philosophy based on worship of the Greek-Roman deity Eris, the goddess of Chaos. Its 'holy book' is the *Principia Discordia*; its principal belief is that both Order and Disorder are illusions; Discordian practice consists of treating everything with humour and absurdity. It has been compared to both **Zen Buddhism** and the **Church of the SubGenius**.

Divination This works by regarding synchronicity or meaningful coincidence as the rule of reality, as opposed to the exception. By learning to read the meaningful connections, one can make all events and things reflect all other events and things in the past, present and future. Some methods of divination are: *Augury* - by the behaviour of birds; *Bletonism* - by currents of water; *Capnomancy* - by smoke; *Ceromancy* - by hot wax; dropped in water; *Lithomancy* - by stones; *Pyromancy* - by looking into a fire.

Dord A nonsense word that was accidentally added to the 1934 edition of Websters International Dictionary; an editor's note reading "D or d, cont./ Density" and meant to be added to the definition for 'density' was misinterpreted by the printer. The mistake went unnoticed for fifteen years.

Dowsing This is the use of a forked hazel or willow branch, or a pendulum, to find things or answer questions. The hazel branch is used to find water or lines of power (ley lines), and the pendulum to answer questions. A pendulum can be used to find things using a map.

Dreams and Dreaming Dreaming is an altered state of consciousness when we can wander freely in our subconscious and imagine what we will. Here we can work out our problems and are given answers, which in many cases are symbolic. The best ways of understanding them is to think what they suggest and mean to you rather than reading interpretation books which often have conflicting meanings for the same thing. We each have an average of about 1000 dreams a year. Lucid dreaming is when we can control what happens in our dreams, rather like astral travelling.

Dragon To the Chinese, the Dragon is the genius of strength and goodness. He is the spirit of change and therefore of Life itself. In the spring he goes into the sky; in the autumn he buries himself in the watery depths. He covers himself with mud at the autumn equinox and emerges in the spring - announcing his awakening by the renewal of nature's energies. There are three main species of Dragon: the *Lung* which is the most powerful and inhabits the sky; The *Li* which is hornless and lives in the sea; the *Chiao* which is scaly and lives in marshes and dens in the mountains.

Druid Celtic priest. The philosophy of the Celts was that neither matter, energy nor the reincarnating soul can be destroyed. They had three circles of being, the inner or central source (*Abred*), the outer circle - the Divine Realm (*Keugant*) and (*Gwenved*) the middle circle containing the perfect happiness of ordinary life.

Ectoplasm *Ectos* - outside, *Plasmo* - to shape (Greek) This substance, midway between matter and spirit is produced by mediums (usually through their mouths) to make apparitions visible to people. The production of ectoplasm usually leaves the medium drained of energy. Touching the ectoplasm or the medium is said to be very dangerous to the medium; doing so can cause harm, and possibly death, to her/him. Mediums who are able to form ectoplasm are called physical mediums. In the past, several such mediums were exposed as frauds; today, there are only a handful who still give seances.

Egypt In Egypt we encounter the roots of the entire Western tradition and also the roots of Greek philosophy and science. The Egyptians believed that life was a miracle and they worshipped creation as a product of magic. They drew no lines of difference, other than focus, in the degree or quality of consciousness between God, animal and man. They did not make the slightest division between religion, magic, science or art. They regarded the gods as entities to be understood so that they could be used to maintain or alter the natural course of things.

El This is a very ancient word with a long history. It has a common origin with several other ancient words in other languages - all of them with a common significant meaning: the Sumerian EL meant 'brightness' or 'shining'; the Akkadian ILU meant 'the bright one'; the Babylonian ELLU meant 'the shining one'; the Old Welsh ELLYL meant 'a shining being'; the Old Irish AILLIL meant 'shining'; the English ELF meant 'a shining being' (from the Anglo-Saxon AELF)'; the Old Cornish EL meant 'an angel'.

Electromagnetism The phenomenon which results from and depends upon the relationship between electricity and magnetism.

Elementals Non-human nature spirits and devas which care for animal life and vegetation and are linked with the elements. There are six main groups: *Salamanders* - Spirits of Fire; *Sylphs* - Spirits of the Air; *Fauns or Satyrs* - Spirits of Animal Life; *Undines* - Spirits of Water and Rivers; *Dryads* - Spirits of Vegetation; and *Gnomes* - Spirits of the Earth.

Ennead The Ennead was a group of nine deities worshipped by the Egyptians at Heliopolis. The group usually consisted of the sun god Atum, his children Shu and Tefnut, their children Geb and Nut, and their children Osiris, Isis, Seth, and Nephthys. Sometimes Horus (the son of Isis and Osiris) was included. The **Ogdoad** were a similar group of Egyptian gods and goddesses.

Energy In a metaphysical sense, energy is one of two separate and distinct forms or expressions of reality. In practical application, energy describes the dispersion of power. Some forms of energy such as electrical energy, can to a degree be controlled. Heat is the lowest form of energy - heat is wasted energy. Energy is convertible to matter and vice versa.

Eratosthenes of Cyrene (c.276-c.194 BC) was a Greek mathematician and astronomer. He was the first to calculate the Earth's diameter and axis tilt, created the first map of the known world and created a calendar system with leap days.

Escape Velocity The speed needed to escape from the gravitational pull of a planetary body. In the case of the Earth, the escape velocity is 6.9 miles per second.

E.V.P. Electric Voice Phenomena (Raudive voices) is the term describing the apparent sound of voices on tape when there has been no one physically there speaking. It was discovered by Friedrich Jürgenson, a Swedish opera singer and artisy who found he got voices on tape whilst he was recording birds. Jürgenson (who also heard ghostly voices without using a tape recorder and received telepathic messages from outer space) wrote a book about his experiences in 1964, which was read by Dr

Konstantin Raudive, a psychologist and professor at a German university. Roudive studied and researched the subject, making over 70,000 tapes. Eventually concluding that the voices were the voices of the dead, he always rejected the possibility that his tapes were capturing errant radio broadcasts. However, the one time he agreed to record inside a Faraday cage (which blocks radio signals) his tapes recorded nothing.

Extra-Solar planets These are planets orbiting around other stars, and astronomers have detected thousands so far. Many are giant planets as large as or larger than Jupiter (the largest planet in our Solar System), but some are smaller - the least massive planet found so far is only twice the mass of our Moon. Such planets are detected by measuring the tiny 'wobbles' in stars' movements caused by the gravitational effects of orbiting bodies. The nearest exoplanets orbit Proxima Centauri, 4.2 light years away and the closest star to the Sun

Fate When we are born, our book of life only has chapter headings with no words except for chapter one - our birth experience. The rest is filled in by us on our journey through life. The headings of the chapters determine the areas we have to experience, but how we do this depends on our own attitudes and understanding. The book develops as you go along; fate provides a framework and you paint the pictures. The forces of fate form the material for your life and they can push you in a direction. This pushing can bring you to the end of one chapter and into another. We are responsible for who and what we are and if you don't like this then it is up to you to bring about the change. Fate can help direct us by putting us in the right place at the right time. It is up to us to read the directions carefully and go down the right road.

Fates Greek and Roman myth explaining an individual's birth, life and death patterns. There were three of them: *Clotho* - spinner of life's thread; *Lachesis* - measurer of the thread; *Atropis* - cutter of the thread. Fate herself was *Moira*, the oldest power in the universe.

Feng Shui Ancient Chinese system of harmonious surroundings which bring health, happiness and prosperity. On the one hand it can be seen as a way of interpreting the forces of the cosmos, and on the other an approach to well-ordered living in harmony with one's environment. Feng Shui is the acknowledgement of the powers of the natural world and an attempt to live in harmony with all the hidden forces therein. By conflicting with the natural order, the Tao, you disturb the balance of Yin and Yang, the two fundamental forces of the universe.

Gaia The Greek earth goddess, also the name given to the single organism comprised by the atmosphere, biosphere and lithosphere of our planet, thus seeing the planet as a holistic, self-regulating entity.

Galactic Centre The Milky Way's gravitational centre, located in the Sagittarius constellation, 27,000 light years away from earth. This has a high concentration of stars similar but older than that of our sun, so it is logical to presume that life would have developed in such a planetary system millions of years before it developed on our own planet. A supermassive black hole, known as Sagittarius A* lies at the centre and recent research suggests there may be many more smaller black holes there.

Galactic Year Time taken by the Sun and its accompanying solar system to make a complete orbit round the centre of the home galaxy - about 225 to 250 million Earth-years.

Ghosts Ghosts can be a magnetic memory in the atmosphere that can be triggered by some people via their energy levels, causing a type of video replay in the air. Other ghosts or apparitions are earthbound spirits tied to earth for various reasons and who need the help of a medium to get onto the astral levels.

The God Particle This is the popular name given to the Higgs boson, an elementary sub-atomic particle discovered in 2012. The particle has nothing to do with any god; the name comes from the title of a sensationalist book on the subject and physicists themselves never use it. See also the **Oh My God! Particle**.

Gods and Goddesses Gods and Goddesses are said to be supreme beings that have power over nature and human fortunes. In all religions, God is seen to be the supreme being and creator of the universe. Therefore the idea that a supreme power of god is the way that man, who represents the microcosm, can relate to the higher power in the macrocosm. Man needs this intermediary stage to be at one with the universe and in various religions acknowledges many different gods and goddesses (the Trinity for Christians, Krishna and Jambavati for Hindus, Zeus and Hera for the ancient Greeks, the Horned God and White Lady for the Wiccans, Isis and Osiris for the ancient Egyptians). All gods have one thing in common, they are considered to be the masters of the universe and human destiny. There are lesser gods who are supposed to make it possible to approach 'God' with personal requests. This does not just occur in Paganism - Christians approach their god through saints, apostles and martyrs. Einstein defined God as 'the ultimate natural order'.

Hades Originally the name given by the Greeks to the God of the Dead and ruler of the underworld, where the shades of dead humans and mythological creatures were thought to be confined. He was a son of Cronos and Rhea, brother of Zeus and Poseidon, Hera, Hester and Demeter, and the consort of his niece Persephone, the daughter of Zeus and Demeter. He was often referred to as Pluto. However, he was not much worshipped by the Greeks as his reign was confined to the dead, therefore he possessed no interest in the living. When the Universe had originally been shared out, Pluto had been given the underworld, Zeus the sky and Poseidon the sea. Hades is now more commonly thought of as the location of the Underworld, rather than its god.

Harvest Moon The full moon nearest to the Autumn Equinox.

Healing Healing is brought about by our own magnetism, power and energy which can be finely tuned and then directed towards another person through love; and by opening ourselves up to the cosmic force which pours through us all from the crown of our heads and can be manifested through our hands. You do not have to have faith to be healed. Everyone is a potential healer and everyone is capable of healing themselves. With visualisation the healing power of the mind can be accessed and influenced; when we have positive emotions, the white blood cells which are our defence against disease increase. The body is just a machine (a temple for the soul) and when pushed to its limits or not serviced in the correct way by proper diet and rest, it breaks down. Parts can stop working and rust away. Looking after ourselves is the first aspect of healing.

Hermetic Doctrine 'As above, so below' comes from *The Emerald Tablet of Hermes*, a text whose origins are from the 8th century or earlier, stating that God is all, God is within, giving life and inspiring all that we do. These were sacred texts of a minor sect who worshipped the Egyptian god Thoth, the ibis headed god, divider of time, law giver and counter of the stars. He was identified with Hermes, the Greek god concerned with wisdom and learning. Hermes was thought to have written these sacred texts, hence the name 'Hermes Trismegistos' (Thrice Greatest). The first Hermes was in all probability a pharaoh, who wrote much on magic and is referred to in the Egyptian Book of the Dead as a wise physician and magician.

Holy Grail In Celtic myth the Grail belonged to the god Bran in the form of a magical cauldron capable of bringing people back to life. Later Christians saw it as a large dish which contained many magical powers, and much later it became the cup used by Jesus to perform the rites of the Last Supper. This cup was brought to Britain by Joseph of Arimathea and thought of as a sacred talisman. It was then lost around Glastonbury and later one of King Arthur's knights, Sir Percival, found it and went through many spiritual trials in order to understand its power. The Grail has been lost since then. It symbolises the search for wisdom and immortality.

Humours   Hippocrates (fifth century BC), in an attempt to explain the nature of humanity, put forward the four humours - blood, phlegm, black bile and yellow bile, and four temperaments - sanguine, phlegmatic, melancholic, choleric. Good health depended on the correct mixture of these and an imbalance brought on illnesses.

Hunter's Moon This is the Full Moon that follows the **Harvest Moon**.

I-Ching This is the Chinese way of prediction and divination which is done by casting yarrow stalks or coins to calculate a set of hexagrams which are then looked up in the Book Of Changes to give an answer to a particular problem. There are 8 basic trigrams in the I-Ching, which are combined to make 64 different forms of hexagrams. The I-Ching has been used as a form of divination in China for at least 5,000 years and quite possibly longer. The fundamental idea of the I Ching is that human nature and cosmic order are one.

IDIC stands for Infinite Diversity in Infinite Combination. The concept first appeared in a Star Trek episode aired in the US in October 1968, where it was presented as a cornerstone of Vulcan philosophy. This quote from the episode sums it up: *The glory of creation is in its infinite diversity. And the ways our differences combine to create meaning and beauty.* This idea was adopted as the guiding philosophy of the **Church of All Worlds**, which had been formally chartered as a religion in the United

States - the first earth-based faith so recognised - on 4 March 1968, a few months before the episode aired.

Ides The 15th of March, May, July, October, and the 13th of every other month in the ancient Roman calendar.

Illuminati This was a secret society founded in Bavaria in 1776 by Adam Weishaupt, an academic and philosopher. Weishaupt, an atheist, was concerned by the tight grip that the various churches had on society at the time and formed a group of fellow-thinkers to spread rationalist and scientific thinking. Because secularists were discriminated against and sometimes persecuted, members had to be secretive and use aliases and secret signs. Curiously, despite the group's dedication to free-thought, membership was restricted to Christians. And although originally against Freemasonry, Weishaupt eventually decided that he would get more members if he affiliated his group with them and adopted their rituals. In time, the group split into various warring sects, some of whom were recklessly open about their intention to bring down the Church and the monarchy. In 1785, an alarmed Bavarian government banned all secret societies; Adam Weishaupt fled the country and his Illuminati group disbanded. Enemies, however, continued to paint them as secret conspirators, claiming that they had masterminded the French Revolution and various other anti-monarchist rebellions. This has lead to modern ideas about an all-powerful secret society manipulating world events.

Kabalah The foundation of most Egyptian and western systems of magic, consisting of Sacred

Jewish teachings or secret knowledge which has been passed down by word of mouth since Abraham. It is a complete symbolic system concerning angels, demons and magic. The teachings were written in Hebrew in the first century in the Book of Creation by a rabbi who was originally a shepherd. He was martyred by the Romans in AD 138, and was said to have had 24,000 followers. Probably the greatest book on Kabbalism was written in Spain around 1290 - the *Zohar* or *Sefer-ha-Zohar* (Book of Splendour or Book of Lights) which states: 'Love unites the highest and lowest stages and lifts everything to the stage where all must be one.' The Kabalah is depicted as a tree of life in which all parts are interdependent. It has 10 spheres and when combined these represent all that exists in the universe, the cosmos being a living entity in which all parts rely on each other.

Kemetism is the modern revived form of the ancient Egyptian religion (Kemet is the ancient name for Egypt). Followers of Kemetism generally worship the traditional Egyptian gods - Maat, Bast, Anubis, Sekhmet and Thoth - but recognise the existence of every god. Kemetic worship takes the form of prayer and the decoration of altars, but there are no set guidelines for rituals.

Kirlian photography A type of photography that is said to detect and display auras, discovered in 1939 by Russian inventor Semyon Kirlian. An object is put into contact with a photographic plate that is connected to a high-voltage source; the image subsequently recorded on the plate always shows a striking, radiating corona, often in a variety of colours. Many claim this is the life-force aura surrounding all living things; however, this "aura" is actually a simple electrical discharge produced by the attached electrical wiring and it can form around any object, alive or dead.

Knots Knots represent a sealed bargain. Religious orders tie knots around their waist signifying commitment to their god. Knotting and binding during initiation signifies that the initiate is 'bound' to do good. A continuous knot takes the form of a figure eight which represents infinity. If you untie a knot you will have solved a mystery within yourself. Alexander the Great cut the Gordian Knot, which no-one had been able to undo, and it became a symbol of his power.

Lemuria Edgar Cayce in one of his readings claimed the Mu were the people of Lemuria, a sunken continent which, according to legend, preceded Atlantis, existing somewhere in either the Indian or Pacific Oceans.

Ley Lines Ley lines are lines of natural energy that flow along the earth's surface. They were first described in a book by Alfred Watkins in 1921 and can be found by dowsing. *Ley* is a Saxon word which means 'alignment', and these lines of psychic power usually pass through ancient sites and monuments and have been found to line up world-wide. Animal tracks and the migration paths of birds usually follow ley lines. They can be physically felt, like an invisible current of energy.

Light Light is a type of radiation which travels at 186,300 miles per second. It is the visible electromagnetic radiation that stimulates the sense of sight. Light can be manipulated for use in delicate surgery and as a terrible weapon of destruction in the form of the LASER (**L**ight **A**mplification by **S**timulated **E**mission of **R**adiation). In astronomical measurement, a light year is the distance travelled by light in one year - 9.46 trillion kilometres or 5.88 trillion miles.

Love Love is the most powerful thing in the universe and how we tap in to it depends upon our own consciousness and spiritual development; sharing on all levels is to love; being intimate is a demonstration of love. If you learn to love yourself then love will come to you, drawn to you by the energy your unselfish self love is giving out.

The Macrocosm and Microcosm The macrocosm can be compared to a massive oak tree that has been growing longer than anyone can remember. This tree has lived through many changes in its lifetime. The microcosm is like the acorns from the tree which get scattered on the ground. They can be a great distance from the tree, scattered by the wind and animals but still containing part of the tree (if only in the acorn's genetic code). Gradually these acorns become other trees, gathering new experiences with the strength and qualities of their parent already present.

The macrocosm is all the universe, galaxies, stars, planets and all the space in between. The microcosm is a miniature version and is the atoms, molecules, cells, subatomic particles and all the space in between them; we call this man. Therefore the universe is like a human organism on a giant scale and man a miniature copy, like the oak tree and the acorn. The idea is that man is a perfect replica of the macrocosm and that by exploring and using his own individual potential he can grow enough to

204

understand and blend in with the universe as a whole, as the potential of an acorn to become an oak tree. The universe used to be a mass of energy filled with life potential or life essence in total harmony with itself; gradually the forces of change built up and the whole thing exploded sending millions of pieces all over the universe. One of these pieces is mankind, which vibrates with the same energy as the original mass but is separate (like the acorn when it falls off the tree). Some of the pieces of the essence divided over and over, while some formed into individual spirits which experience more intense forms of separateness by entering into dense physical matter; each bit had a small fragment of the original mass in it that vibrated with the same Life essence that is in every living thing.

We have all the knowledge and experience of all that original mass inside us; but we all grow our separate lives as well as having computer-like records of everything that has gone on before stored in us. When this life essence has been expanded to its capacity for knowledge, then it will gradually start to contract over millions of years and all the separate parts will come together again. But, because of the extra experience of all the bits that have been flying around the universe learning and experiencing, it will be different. The big new oak tree it will reform into will have lots of different branches added to it.

Magic   Magic is the ability, through training and natural skill, to manipulate a little known natural force to achieve changes in the magician's or other people's consciousness and to effect changes in the physical environment. This force is neutral in its normal state and can be used for good or ill. Magic is the conscious application of the laws of nature to utilise this force. The doctrines of magic and their relationship were summed up by Paracelcus (who was alive in the fifteenth century and has been described as the father of modern medicine; his magical view of the world was that human life is inseparable from that of the universe) as follows: "*The astral currents created by the imagination of the macrocosm act upon the microcosm and produce certain stages in the latter, and likewise the astral currents, produced in the imagination and the will of man produces certain states in the external Nature; and these currents may reach far, because the power of the imagination reaches as far as thought can go. The physiological processes taking place in the bodies of living beings are caused by their astral currents and the changes taking place in the great organism of Nature are caused by the astral currents of Nature as a whole. The astral currents (mankind or Nature) act upon each other, either consciously or unconsciously; and if this is properly understood it will cease to appear incredible that the mind of man may produce changes in the universal mind, or that evil may be changed into good by the powers of faith. Heaven is a field into which the imagination of man throws the seeds*".

Mary Baker Eddy (1821 - 1910) was the founder of Christian Science. She taught that all matter and suffering is an illusion and that there is no personal God. Her rejection of hygiene, doctors and medicine for healing was not only because of her belief that sickness arises solely out of spiritual disturbance, but also because Jesus didn't use any of those for healing; she also taught that nobody had any need to learn about health. These beliefs have unfortunately led to many avoidable deaths.

Meditation A means of allowing the deepest self to speak. Meditation is really only deep thinking, concentrated and free from distractions. It has an energising process.

Miracles These are a flow of energy taking their natural form without any hindrance from man.

Mormonism Also known as the Latter Day Saints movement, this was founded by Joseph Smith in the 1820s. Smith claimed he had been directed by an angel to the burial place of some golden plates that were inscribed in an unknown language; he was able to translate this writing, which turned out to be *The Book of Mormon*, the Mormons' sacred book. This described how numerous Israelite families travelled from pre-Christian Palestine and populated the Americas; Jesus also travelled to America after His resurrection. Mormons regard themselves as Christian and also hold the Bible as sacred.

Names The ancient Egyptians believed that the name of a person was one of their 'bodies', if you didn't have a name you couldn't 'go on' when you died, and you fell into the void. If you change your name, you change your vibrations. Most magicians assume different names because our names rule the nature of the events that gravitate towards us.

Nirvana Buddha said that there is a way out of the endless cycle of birth, death and rebirth: to step off the wheel of Karma into Nirvana. In Sanskrit it means 'blown out' or extinguished'. Rebirth being the result of desire, freedom from rebirth signifies the removal of desire; so the flame is extinguished. Nirvana is a state of complete calm where cleansed souls dwell, free from space and time.

Numerology The ancient scientific study of the connection between numbers and events in our everyday world. It was practised successively in the Vedic tradition of ancient India, by the ancient Chaldeans and Greeks and more recently by western numerologists. Numerologists can make a numerical analysis of a person's name and birthdate and can then describe some of his or her important personality traits and point out any special potential for achievement. 1999 saw a very rare numerological event - on the 19th November, every digit of the date was an odd number (19/11/1999). This will not happen again until 3111 AD!

Ogdoad This is a group of eight deities that were worshipped in Egypt's Old Kingdom, from 2686 to 2134 BC, centring around the city of Hermopolis. It consisted of four male and four female divinities, each pair representing different aspects of the four primordial elements (primordial water, infinity, invisibility and darkness). Eventually, these eight combined to give birth to Ra, the Sun god.

The **Oh-My-God! Particle** This is not a joke. On the evening of the 15th October 1991, astrophysicists in Utah detected a space particle travelling at an astonishing and unprecedented speed of 99.999+% of the speed of light. Since then, around 15 other similar particles have been detected, all of them apparently originating somewhere within the Orion constellation. See also the **God Particle**.

Parallel Universes/Multiverse/Many Worlds This is a theory that other universes exist alongside our own.

The concept has existed for millennia - the ancient Greek philosophy of **Atomism** proposed that an infinite number of other worlds existed alongside our own; in 1952 Erwin Schrödinger said that his equations showed that "multiple histories" could exist simultaneously. However, many physicists have argued against the idea, on the basis that it's a metaphysical concept that - while interesting - cannot be either proved or disproved.

Philosophy Philosophy is an organised system of belief and knowledge which seeks to explain the universe, the natural forces operating in the universe, the purpose of existence, the correct manner of organising and living one's life and our relation to the world and each other.

Precession of the Equinoxes This is caused by the gravitational attraction of the Sun and Moon on the bulge at the Earth's equator. Thus there is a slow backwards movement of the Equinoctial point along the Sun's apparent path amongst the stars during the year which is caused by the tilting of the Earth's axis, although this yearly increase is only 50 inches. The complete retrograde (backwards) cycle of the Equinoctial Points around the path of the Sun among the stars takes about 25,800 years. It is because of precession that astrology is frequently challenged by those sceptics who think the zodiacal signs are the constellations of the same name and who point out that when astrologers say that the Sun is in Aries 0° degrees (at the spring equinox) it is actually 5 degrees into the constellation of Pisces (at the present time).

Precognition The personal knowledge, not founded on prior knowledge or events, that some future event is to occur. Precognition can come in dreams, thoughts, feelings or sensations and can apply to people or situations such as fires or earthquakes.

Psychokinesis   This is the ability to move objects using only the power of the mind.

Pyramids   Pyramids have been built in many parts of the world., not just Egypt. They can be found in the Middle East, North Africa, Central America, Mexico, China, Indonesia and India. The earliest pyramidal structures were the ziggurats in Mesopotamia (modern Iraq) which were built around 3000 BC. Most pyramid structures were used as temples, and pyramids built solely as tombs are fairly rare.

Quantum Mechanics   The theory which describes the rules by which sub-atomic particle interaction can be explained.   It states that energy is parcelled as separate quanta (plural of quantum) which take part in atomic and subatomic interactions. It deals with Heisenburg's Uncertainty Principle which states that there is a limit to how much one can know about subatomic interactions - one can only deal in probabilities. For instance, if you look down a microscope at a leaf you see a leaf - the leaf is the same if you look at it or not. If you look at a sub-atomic particle you don't see it as it was before you looked at it, so you don't really know what it was like.

Reincarnation   The belief of reincarnation is that a soul leaves the body on physical death and goes to the astral level to rest and heal from the lessons and pains it has gone through in life and consolidate its knowledge before being reborn to learn further lessons and life experiences. Our Astrological sign can give us indications of what we have to learn in our present life. If our astrological sign is Fire then we have to learn the lesson of love, its power mystery and magic; if it is Earth we have to learn to gain mastery over physical matter and to serve others; if it is Air (the most subtle signs) we have to learn the ability to stand outside and observe; and if it is Water we have to learn to control our emotions so as to find peace. Plato, Emerson, Edison, Shaw, Jung, Nietzche and Shopenhauer all accepted reincarnation.

Remote Viewing An ability similar to clairvoyance whereby individuals can supposedly view specific locations, objects and events that can be anywhere - other cities, countries or even planets. The USA spent 20 million dollars on Project Stargate (a scientific project researching remote viewing), and psi research over a period of 20 years, but concluded that it simply didn't work.

Rosicrucians A 17th century group of monks who claimed to have found secret and powerful mystical knowledge. The original founder in the 14th or 15th century was a German, Christian Rosenkreutz (Rosy Cross), who it is claimed, lived to 106 years of age. He was educated by monks and when young went on a pilgrimage to the Holy Land before going on to Arabia and Egypt. He learnt much along the way before returning to Germany. For a while he became a hermit, before forming the order of The Rosy Cross with four friends. They invented a secret language and were concerned with medical matters, particularly healing. The Rosicrucian Order exists today and is a world wide educational and philosophical organisation.

Scientology Also known as Dianetics, this is a 'science of mind' invented by the sci-fi writer L. Ron Hubbard. It is partly derived from classical psychoanalysis; the Scientology terms *analytical mind, reactive mind, engrams* and *clearing* are used in place of the psychoanalytical terms *conscious mind, unconscious mind, trauma* and *catharsis,* but mean the same thing. Hubbard thought that many illnesses are caused by engrams (traumas) occurring before birth and claimed to have cured himself of several ailments by 'clearing' himself of such engrams (i.e., cathartically recalling the original traumas). The Church of Scientology was incorporated in America in 1953, when the engram concept was developed to incorporate past lives going back many millennia. In Scientology teachings, each individual human being is said to consist of a transient genetic entity (the physical body) inhabited by an eternal 'Thetan'. A Thetan is an ancient soul-being from another star-system trapped on this planet by engrams that originated in the primitive life-forms that were our distant Earth ancestors; it has been helplessly reincarnating in physical form over and over again for untold millions of years. Clearing all these engrams will, it is said, enable each person's inner Thetan to regain full consciousness and escape materiality.

Serendipity This is the art of making a fortunate discovery by accident. The word was coined by the author Horace Walpole on January 28th 1754. The exact date is from a letter he wrote to his friend Horace Mann, explaining that he had coined the word from a Persian fairy story called *The Three Princes of Serendip,* whose heroes "*were always making* *discoveries, by accidents and sagacity, of things they were not in quest of."*

Shaman A Siberian word for medicine man, magician and priest. A shaman can be male or female and can commune with the gods and command the spirits.

Solar Wind A continuous stream of particles emitted by the Sun.

Solomon According to the Old Testament, he was a king of Israel, noted for his great wisdom and wealth; he ruled from about 970 to 931 BC. Both Jews and Muslims regard him as a major prophet and many legends have been built up around him; for example, he was said to transport his armies on flying carpets. He was also said to be a great magician; many magical amulets and seals bear his name.

The Soul The soul is the communicative centre that looks after all our needs so that our inner spirit can gain wisdom and knowledge. It absorbs all our experience: mental, physical and spiritual and sorts them out so that the pure spirit which it surrounds doesn't receive any rubbish. The soul is a spiritual entity, not a physical one, and it cannot be seen. The spirit or life force is deep inside our dense physical bodies and the soul surrounds this, making sure that our spirit is in the best condition to evolve on to a higher vibration so that the spirit (life force or energy centre) can function more clearly and efficiently through our bodies.

Sub-Atomic Particles The whole of our physical
Sufism is a mystical form of Islam whose followers seek spiritual perfection and direct contact with God via prayer, meditation, study and - in the case of **Dervishes** - dance. Sufism originated in the first

century after Islam was established, probably as a backlash against the materialism and political ambitions of early Muslim rulers. Sufis aren't a separate sect and any Muslim can be a Sufi.

Superstitions Superstitions or omens have been with us since ancient times. Once the province of the fortune tellers and soothsayers as interpretative messages from the gods, they are now everyday folklore, varying in meaning in different parts of the country.

Here are a few:

To bring apple blossom into the house means you're bringing sickness in. Bees should always be told of a death in the family (especially if it is their keeper), by putting strips of black cloth on their hives and leaving them out a bit of food from the funeral meal. After a beekeeper's death, his bees have been known to swarm on his house and grave.

A spark on the wick of a candle indicates a letter is coming, a big glow on the wick means money and a blue flame means that there are spirits present.

If a hairy caterpillar creeps on you it's lucky and you're supposed to throw it over your shoulder - with care!

A hare running through the village streets means there will be a fire.

Coal has always been carried for luck in many situations Soldiers in the first world war often had a small piece in their pockets and robbers in past times always carried a bit.

To hear a cuckoo before the swallow indicates a bad year ahead, but if you hear the cuckoo for the first time on Easter Sunday morning, all will be well for you in the coming year.

Elephants are considered very lucky. If you have an elephant ornament in a room it should always be facing the door, as elephants are supposed to get angry if they can't see what's going on.

If you see a feather lying on the ground, always stick it upright in the earth and this will bring you luck. Passing a hay wagon also signify good luck.

If the sole of your foot itches it means you're going to go somewhere you've never been before.

To see goats on the way to a new venture signifies success and to hear grasshoppers singing means a lucky journey. To drop your key when going to open your door is a sign that you will be moving.

If a knife or scissors fall and stick into the floor, wish whilst pulling them out and your wish will come true.

Ladybirds mean luck and signify visitors, so must not be killed.

Leaves blowing into your house is a sign of luck coming in. Mice are a sign of personal danger.

Cutting your nails on a Monday morning is most fortunate and you should expect a present within the week.

Carry a nutmeg in your pocket for backache.

Owls have always been thought of as ill omens from time immemorial, perhaps they can indeed sense death approaching.

Rosemary and Rowan are plants which provide protection.

If your boot or shoe laces keep coming undone there is a surprise coming your way.

All spiders are lucky, the little red ones are for money and the long legged ones are for general good fortune, so never kill a spider.

It is most unlucky to cross on the stairs and one person should always go backwards and wait.

Swallows building their nests around your house bring luck to the house. Toads and frogs mean luck.

T'ai Chi Chinese philosophers refer to the origin of all created things as the T'ai Chi. This is symbolised in their books by the whole figure representing the T'ai Chi and the divided portions called Yin and Yang. This is the Chinese symbol of the duality of nature and life, and the picture shows the passive and active forces of the universe. Yin is female and negative and Yang is male and positive; between them they cover all types of existence and all types of relating. Their basic rule is that they obey life's only certainty - change. The circle represents the origin of all created things and when split into two represents life reduced to its primary constituents, the male and female principles. It is the essence of extreme virtue and perfection in heaven and earth, men and all things. From the T'ai Chi or ultimate principle, composed of the Yin and Yang (male and female principles) man is enriched at birth with the possession of the five virtues - Benevolence, Purity, Property, Wisdom and Truth.

Telepathy This is the ability to talk mind to mind with someone else without any physical contact.

Theosophy The Theosophical Society was founded in the USA in 1875 by Helena P. Blavatsky (1831-1891) and Colonel Henry Olcott (1832-1907); they later went to Madras in India to establish the headquarters. She was Russian, and after a brief marriage at 17, left her husband General NV Blavatsky and travelled in Egypt, India and Tibet. Henry Olcott was a barrister and an agriculturalist who was interested in the occult. Helena is believed to have met and been guided by Masters or adepts. Her first publication was an attempt to equate ancient mythology and religion. Her most famous work *The Secret Doctrine* caused a stir when it was published as it incorporated eastern teachings which were a strange new concept for the Western world. Theosophy taught that we have four bodies: the Physical, the Astral, the Etheric and the Self; it also discussed religion, science and philosophy in a completely new way for the time.

Thought This, after love, is the strongest power in the universe, everything comes from thought: philosophy, art, invention and healing. The mind is immensely powerful and if you think strongly about anything and have single-mindedness you will eventually get it. Thoughts of love are very powerful because love comes from the spirit or energy source inside us that is part of the macrocosm and the microcosm that is ourselves. Everything we do or have has been created by thought.

UFO Many people think that 'UFO' is just another name for a 'flying saucer' or other alien object. In fact, the initials stand for Unidentified Flying Object. It is just that - unidentified - until it becomes an IFO (Identified Flying Object).

World Contact Day Held on the 15th March annually, this was first declared in March 1953 by an organisation called the International Flying Saucer Bureau. On this day everybody is asked to send a telepathic message of friendship and welcome to all aliens in Earth's vicinity.

The Wow! Signal This is a true scientific mystery. On August 15 1977, Dr. Jerry R. Ehman was working on a SETI project at Ohio State University, analysing radio waves picked up from the Sagittarius region of deep interstellar space. Noticing a sudden 72-second spike in a continuous narrowband radio signal, he drew a circle around it on the printout and scribbled "WOW!" next to it. It has never been repeated since, so what was it? A signal from some extraterrestrial civilisation? A top-secret secret military operation in space? Or just a malfunctioning radio in the next room? There are plenty of ideas, but nobody knows for sure. Perhaps we'll find out one day....

Yin and Yang This is the Chinese representation of the duality of life and the symbol shows the passive and active forces of the universe. Yin is female and negative and Yang is male and positive; between them they cover all types of existence and all types of relating. Their basic rule is that life's only certainty is hope.

Zen Buddhism This is a fusion of Buddhism and Taoism that began in the 6thC AD. Zen practitioners attempt to encounter and understand the meaning of life directly, without the filters of thought and language; this is called enlightenment and is to be achieved through meditation and the practice of 'mindfulness' and other spiritual disciplines. In Zen, all humans are capable of finding enlightenment within themselves, without the mediation of priests, teachers or gurus.

Odd Facts You Probably Never Knew!

• US park ranger Roy Sullivan was struck by lightning seven times and survived; the last strike happened shortly after the 22nd time he'd had to fight off a bear with his stick.

• The niece of Kubla Khan agreed to marry any man who beat her at wrestling, but demanded payment in horses if she won. She died unmarried with 100,000 horses.

• In 1940s Britain, children's television shows were shown from 5pm to 6pm, then transmission stopped for an hour to encourage them to go to bed.

• The surface area of a cat, including each hair of its fur, is 100 times that of its skin and is enough to cover a ping-pong table.

• Ping-pong balls were made larger to make the sport better for TV.

• The Elizabethans treated warts by cutting a mouse in half and applying it to the affected part.

• Rats multiply so quickly that in 18 months, one pair of rats could have over million descendants.

• Wearing headphones for just an hour will increase the bacteria in your ear by 700 times.

• Like fingerprints, everyone's tongue print is different.

• The coal, oil and gas we burn each year requires as much organic matter to make as the entire planet grows in roughly 600 years.

• Francesco Morosini, the ruler of Venice between 1688 and 1694, refused to go into battle without his cat by his side.

• The iron carrying oxygen from your lungs to the rest of your body was made when stars exploded.

· The Norwegian word 'fylleangst' means "that unsettling feeling one has the day after drinking when you can't remember what you did while you were drunk".

· A word that can be spelled with only musical notes - A, B, C, D, E, F, G - is called a 'piano word'. The longest one in English is 'cabbage-faced'.

· The Anti-Saccharine Movement of the 1790s was a British attempt to boycott sugar to reduce the profits of slave traders.

· The word 'trumpery' means gaudy, garish, tasteless, vulgar, fakery, fraud, of little value or use.

· J R R Tolkien hated chainsaws for the harm they did to trees; he used to shout 'Orcs!' when he heard one.

• The word 'zemblanity' means "the faculty of making unhappy, unlucky and expected discoveries by design". Coined by novelist William Boyd, it is the autonym (opposite) of serendipity.

· 'Fnord' is an invented word that first appeared in 1965, in the Discordian religious text *Principia Discordia* and was used in a string of satirical novels by Robert Shea and Robert Anton Wilson, where it was an expression of hypnotic command and mind control. It was later taken up by early internet culture to indicate irony, humour, or Surrealism.

"I would rather have questions that can't be answered, than answers that cannot be questioned."
~ Professor Richard Feynman

Solar & Lunar Eclipses in 2023

20th April - Total Solar Eclipse
The total eclipse will only be visible from East Timor and parts of Papua New Guinea and coastal Western Australia. A partial eclipse will be visible from most of South-East Asia, Australia, the South Pacific. southern Indian Ocean and parts of Antarctica.

5th - 6th May 2023 - Penumbral Lunar Eclipse
A penumbral Lunar eclipse is when only the outer part of the Earth's shadow passes over the Moon. The Moon's face only darkens a little, so this type of eclipse can easily be missed.
Visible across almost all of Europe (excepting the British Isles and Sweden), Africa, Asia, Australia, Antarctica and the Indian Ocean.

14th October 2023 - Annular Solar Eclipse
An annular solar eclipse happens when the Moon passes in front of the Sun while at its farthest point from Earth. At that time the Moon appears a little smaller than the Sun; as a result, we see a "ring of fire" around the Moon at totality.
The partial part of the eclipse will be visible in most of the United States, Mexico, and parts of South and Central America; totality will be visible in a narrow band across the South-West USA, parts of Mexico, most of Central America and the North-West parts of South America.

28th - 29th October 2023 - Partial Lunar Eclipse
This will be visible across most of the globe - the whole of Europe, Asia, Africa, most of Australia and parts of North and South America.

In memory of
Caroline Heaney
Founder of the Elfin Diary
1947 - 2011

Transformations
by Thomas Hardy

Portion of this yew
Is a man my grandsire knew,
Bosomed here at its foot:
This branch may be his wife,
A ruddy human life
Now turned to a green shoot.

These grasses must be made Of
her who often prayed,
Last century, for repose;
And the fair girl long ago Whom
I often tried to know May be
entering this rose.

So, they are not underground,
But as nerves and veins abound
In the growths of upper air, And
they feel the sun and rain, And
the energy again
That made them what they were!

Published by Elfin Diaries ©1990 - 2023
www.elfindiaries.co.uk